The Devil Is Clever

A Romanian Christening Party, Dysart, Saskatchewan, 1919.

The Devil Is Clever

A MEMOIR OF MY ROMANIAN MOTHER

BY KENNETH RADU

Harper*Flamingo*Canada

The Devil Is Clever

© 2004 by Kenneth Radu. All rights reserved.

Published by Harper*Flamingo*Canada,
an imprint of HarperCollins Publishers Ltd

First Edition

Author's note:
Some names have been changed to avoid confusion.

Photo on page ii reprinted courtesy of the author.

HarperCollins books may be purchased for educational, business, or sales promotional use through
our Special Markets Department.

HarperCollins Publishers Ltd
2 Bloor Street East, 20th Floor
Toronto, Ontario, Canada
M4W 1A8

www.harpercollins.ca

National Library of Canada Cataloguing in
Publication

Radu, Kenneth
The devil is clever : a memoir / Kenneth Radu. –
1st ed.

ISBN 0-00-200650-2

1. Corches, Annie – Childhood and youth.
2. Romanian Canadians – Saskatchewan – Dysart –
Biography. 3. Dysart (Sask.) – Biography. I. Title.

FC3549.D95Z49 2004   971.24′4   C2003-905627-9

HC 9 8 7 6 5 4 3 2 1

Printed and bound in the United States
Set in Dante

for Diane

Love is not love
Which alters when it alteration finds

SHAKESPEARE

God is great, but the Devil is clever.

—Romanian proverb

Prologue

Prologue

The crow's eye picked out the shiny barrette on the girl's black hair. From the top of the grain elevator, the bird saw it shimmering through the ripples of sunlight like a shard of glass in a stream. Spreading wings easily and wide to catch a current, the crow lifted off the wooden structure rising above the small village and allowed itself to float downward to catch a better glimpse of the desirable object. Flying closer, circling, sensing resistance to its purpose, the bird cawed loudly enough to startle Annie by the train tracks, then tilted its body and veered off to one side. Losing gracefulness in frustrated instinct, the crow flapped over the broad main street of Dysart, Saskatchewan. Annie looked up, the sun hurting her injured eye. She raised a hand to shield it from the glare. So much sky, cool as a frosty windowpane, but clear and blue, without a hint of snow or rain, for it was March, a month prone to the frenzy of contradictions: heat and cold, sun and cloud, rain and snow competing one day to the next for dominance.

She had dressed warmly, although today the sky, despite the chill, lifted high and open with the promise of an early spring. Snow still lay on the ground, piled in dirty mounds by the side of the train station and along the edges of the roads. Her body shivered, not entirely from the cold. One hand hid inside the pocket of her wool coat; the other held an old biscuit tin with a portrait of Queen Alexandra on its dinted lid. Her rose-patterned kerchief had slid off her head and folded itself like a muffler around her neck.

Annie kept looking down the semi-frozen ridges of the dirt road she had walked to reach the station as if expecting someone to pursue and force her to return home. She imagined those leathery-winged, ferocious bird-women she had read about in her school book of stories, who flew after malefactors all over the world, shrieking and striking at them with wings and beaks, compelling them to face the terrible consequences of their crimes. But she knew everyone had gone to the church today, everyone in her family. She saw only a few heavily coated men wearing striped railway caps, one of whom was familiar although Annie did not know his name, men who carried heavy tools like crowbars and iron mallets and worked around the train station and the grain elevator. She was so evidently waiting for the train that they did not bother her after doffing their caps in kindly greetings. A flatbed truck passed on the other side of the tracks, but she did not recognize the driver.

For safety's sake, she wished it were possible to disappear into the sky, invisible even to birds, her apprehension increasing in direct proportion to the train's delay. What if the train was too late? What if her uncle and aunt, having ended their celebrations in the Orthodox church and the ensuing feast across the street in the church hall, drove by and discovered her standing on the station platform? The thought, too horrible to bear, throbbed like the pain behind her eyes. After the accident, the cut on the side of her head had bled to the point of blinding her. It had taken longer than expected to heal, even though no doctor had tended to the wound. For weeks some bruising remained evident around the temple. Since then, she was prone to sudden and ravaging headaches when distressed. The pain seared as if a fiery needle

4

had split the skin of her eye and, penetrating, burned the soft tissues of her brain. There was no medical help for it. God lived in the sky, so the priest said. God looked after the poor and miserable, and suffered the children to come unto Him.

Shielding her eyes against the cutting light of the day, Annie prayed for concealment. She had decided not to wait in the station, although recognizing how prudent that choice would have been, because she wanted to see the great black rumbling dragon of the train chugging toward Dysart. She wanted to see its own magnificent light on the engine beaming like a giant's eye as it approached to carry her away. Of course she was no longer a child and knew it would not fly like a dragon, but it would nonetheless take her into its belly, offering protection of a sort. Provided no one she knew stopped to ask questions. Provided no one stopped at all.

Looking in the distance down the tracks, she heard the slow rumble of the engine before she saw the train's round, almost smiling face under a huff of steam, the station platform trembling under her boots. Annie held her breath, the dream of escape churning into a waking nightmare of apprehension. How slowly the train crawled toward the station, loud and huge, the smell of hot iron steaming in the sky, the screech and tonnage of pistons, engines and wheels vibrating the wooden platform, inexorable and momentous. Her head about to explode, she pressed the portrait of the queen against her breast and, staring down at the sheen of the rails, refused to cry. On such an insubstantial road she would flee. In such a great monster she would run away and celebrate her fifteenth birthday in two months' time with her beloved sister in another place, in another world.

The stationmaster brushed past Annie as steam roared out of the sides and bottom of the dragon. The grain elevator looked as if it would topple and crush her before she escaped to safety. No leathery wings appeared above the engine. The dragon train blocked her view of the road. No one in the village on the other side of the tracks would see her mount the steps to enter the belly of the wonderful monster. How weighted her feet, like blocks of iron. Concentrate, one step at a time, fight back the tears, too old to cry, ignore the needling pain of her eye, slip onto the wooden seat and huddle in the corner, the kerchief covering the head for concealment. My mother, Annie, clutched the biscuit tin of food on that March day in 1928 and never once looked out the window until the train had escaped the avenging furies.

Part One

Mămăligă (Cooked Cornmeal)

2 ½ cups water
1 teaspoon salt
1 cup cornmeal

- Bring water and salt to boil in a large saucepan.
- Add cornmeal slowly, stirring continuously until mixture is thick.
- Remove from heat, and let stand for a few minutes until mixture is firm enough to turn out onto plate.
- Slice using taut thread, and serve with sour cream or syrup.

Serves 6.

CHAPTER I

The Devil lurks behind the cross.

How very subtle and beautiful the land where my mother, Annie, was born. Today, only a sloping grey barn remains, its roof sagging like the sway-back of a decrepit horse. One wonders how it has withstood the blasts of winter winds, the rattle and thunder of summer storms over the decades. Visible from the roads and highways, these grey farm buildings linger on the Saskatchewan landscape, many of them abandoned, boarded-up houses, farm buildings originally designated for specific purposes, now leaning toward collapse, the ruins forming the architectural biographies of an entire people. However melancholy, they are also lovely in their mute, weather-worn way. Annie's original mud-walled home, of course, has since disappeared, washed away by time, changes and prosperity. The front yard of her father's homestead extends to the unpaved grid road, its rutted tracks beaten into permanent shape by years of heavy-wheeled machinery trundling over the terrain. The land is used mostly for pasturage these days. Copses and gullies, sloughs and hillocks, coulees and plains: the land is anything but bare and flat. Its variety and subtlety repay study.

As a woman living in Eastern cities, Annie often sat on the porch, her view obstructed by neighbouring buildings, trees, hydro poles. Never truly at rest, she sat with a bowl on her lap, snapping peas or peeling apples, staring into space, sometimes scanning the sky, hoping for good news from elsewhere. She described the Saskatchewan landscape of her childhood in a hushed and rhythmical voice, as if she were reciting a lyric poem. When she married, Annie moved to her husband's family's home in another region of the province, the Assiniboia district, an area she never learned to love. Less appealing to the eye, less gratifying to the soul, geographically speaking it's a residual extension of the Montana badlands. Indeed, she came close to blaming her husband for the geography, as if his deficiencies of character explained the landscape. The untrammelled view, the largeness of sight, available on the prairies to the human eye, made her impatient with enclosures. The land was inextricably connected with the death and memory of her idealized father. Because of this tremendous sense of loss, no one house satisfied her longing for security and space. Her first childhood home was a generous-spirited shelter, her later adult homes often dreary confinements.

The sky is also to blame in part for her sense of entrapment. Annie eventually left the land, but the sky remained in her heart. So much limitless sky, its character as varied as the land itself, that distance becomes magnified, horizons extend forever beyond reach. "You can breathe there," Annie used to say, especially during the humid heft and wilt of city summers in Ontario. Projecting economic deprivation onto landscape and climate, she felt her life very small indeed because she remembered how large the world used to be. She romanticized, of course, a common failing of the dispossessed, but no one who visits Saskatchewan is unaware of the sweep and drama of the heavens. Annie played in the coulees and fields, along the edges of the sloughs, with her eyes more on the clouds than on the ground rules of the game. From the front door of her aunt's home, which later became Annie's, the driveway slopes down toward the grid road.

Another field stretches on the other side of the road, but the sky swallows that, too. All the agricultural development in the world, which has eliminated much of the flora and fauna and altered the appearance of the original prairie landscape, cannot shrink the sky. Stand and feel oddly humbled and liberated at the same time. The great contradiction of Annie's life is that, born where the possibilities are endless, she grew up in a family situation and economic reality that were constricted and diminished. Her own mind tried hard to reach far, but unable in the deepest psychic sense to achieve a dream, she huddled and narrowed her sights. Yet, wonderful to say, she did not go blind, for she dug into the ground and created a garden. However restricted her range of experience, her knowledge of the land, of how to cultivate, was profound. Soil between the fingers alleviates sorrow. Bombarded by the propaganda of oppressive optimism, we ignore complexities and assume everyone can be victorious, morally impugning those who cannot. Seeing small ironically strengthened Annie's heart. Like the true gardener she was, more often in desire than in fact, she recognized the potential of the seed. Even a negligible, weedy plot of land, if properly tended, can become a paradise. Belief in that possibility helped her survive many a dark year.

Under the enormity of a sky he had never seen in Transylvania, her father, Samson, erected his first shelter, given three years to do so by the terms of the land grant. While building his house and turning the soil six months of the year, he, his wife and two Romanian-born children lived with his brother Simeon. Like many others, the first home was literally built out of the ground, blocks of sod shaped and piled between poplar poles connected with laths. The poles sank two feet deep or more in the ground. Clay mixed with wool was also incorporated into the walls. Unlike his Romanian home, the new dwelling would lack a porch with wooden pillars in which rhombic patterns had been carved. The peaked roof of the rectangular structure was then covered with a combination of thatch, wood and shingles, if the latter were available.

Once dried, the walls inside and out were whitewashed, and Rahila, Annie's mother, hung the Romanian tapestries and blankets she had managed to bring all the way from Transylvania. Stylized birds in the weave of the *tapiserie* and *cuvertură* reminded her of what had been left behind in her native village. Samson had promised to replace her *vârtelniţă*, the spinning wheel so central to the Romanian peasant woman's consciousness. Spinning wheels and looms feature in a great many European tales, "Rumpelstiltskin" being the most commonly known, and become metaphors derived from sources as ancient as the first day of creation. As one Romanian proverb attests, he that labours and thrives *spins* gold. Replacing words with lace, relying on a store of images derived from folklore and desire, Annie rediscovered the artistry of threads in her later life. Lacking a spinning wheel, she wove complicated patterns with the wondrous dexterity of hands and crochet hooks.

Icons of the saints Elizabeth, George, Michael and the Holy Mother were placed where candles could be lit safely out of the reach of children: Niculai, born in 1906, Tenka in 1909, John in 1911 and Mary in 1912. With four children under the age of six, 160 acres to till, so far from her birthplace that Rahila could well have wondered if they had travelled outside of God's field of vision entirely, she found that survival did not leave much time for spiritual rumination or despair. Besides, the church in Dysart confirmed His existence, so all was not lost; she had not been abandoned, however burdened her body and spirit.

Immigrant accounts describe the work and hardships, applauding the heroic courage in the face of disappointment or disaster, but they say virtually nothing of the mind and individual character of the people who did the work. Everyone ends up sounding the same in these stories. We're reading about stereotypes rather than complex, unique human beings. Was everyone courageous, uncomplaining and vigorous? Was everyone grateful to live impoverished lives behind mud walls in a foreign land? Did regrets not occur, wrenching homesickness, even for a land that had taxed, deprived and slaughtered their families? Necessity is the mother of silence, so one can imagine Rahila went about the business of taking care of four children, cooking cornmeal *mămăligă* and, when cabbages were ready, *sarmale*, trying to clean a house that flaked dust in the summer heat or dripped mud when it rained, and hoisted her skirts to help Samson plough the land, keeping her thoughts to herself.

Annie was born May 4, 1913. A home delivery, of course, although a doctor from Cupar, about ten miles away, drove the country roads in his buggy, and in Dysart there was occasionally a nurse who offered assistance during childbirth. When Rahila's waters broke and she knew it was time to deliver the baby, Samson was not expected to hitch the horses and ride to Dysart or Cupar for medical help. Why would such an effort have been necessary in the first place? Peasant women had given birth for centuries, working in the fields until labour pains prevented them, sometimes squatting, their arms held by the married women who surrounded them and prayed to God. *Accouchement* for a peasant woman rarely meant the blessed luxury of several days in bed. Samson called on his neighbours. Within the hour, his fifteen-by-twelve-foot sod house was crowded with the prayers and commands of women, crossing themselves in front of the icons, their heads wrapped in kerchiefs, the symbol of a married woman, and wiping Rahila's brow. Annie was born exactly as she would have been in Romania: delivered by the exertions of her mother in her bed, under the tutelage of experienced peasant women who had endured the agony themselves. Well into the century Annie would repeat her mother's experience, not delivering a child in the hospital until the 1940s. Like mothers everywhere, she was not above blaming her children for labour pains. It's doubtful whether Rahila benefited from anaesthesia of any kind. Rarely was chloroform handy on their larder shelves, in any case.

Using description as a metaphoric stick to beat gratitude into her children, Annie liked to say she was born in a mud house and we were lucky we hadn't been. This is more true than not. Her memory of the building was faulty, if only because she spent more time outside than within. But Samson did live there until his death, reaping and improving from one year to the next. My mother told me a story that says something about her spirit and her memory, how she hung on to extraordinary details of beauty in the midst of desolation.

Her father had cut a small square opening in the sod wall, fitted a window frame in it and covered it with glass purchased from the Hudson's Bay outlet in Fort Qu'Appelle to let the morning sun shine through at that end of the house. His second wife apparently had found the interior too dark. Streaming through the window on a diagonal beam, the light spread over one lower corner section of the whitewashed mud wall, dry as plaster. One spring a tremendous event happened, which excited Annie so much that she wanted to tell someone, except she knew it was always better to say nothing than to reveal anything. Her stepmother frowned upon overexuberant expressions of happiness, placing no trust in good feeling. "You can laugh now," Annie often heard her say to Samson, "but that doesn't get the work done." Her father laughed at least once a day, sometimes to himself while hammering a horse's shoe or yoking the oxen to the plough. Her stepmother's smile was like the weak tea that she fed to the new baby by dipping a corner of a flower sack in her cup and letting Eva suck on it.

Green shoots appeared in the patch of sun. Annie counted them—seven shoots in four different places at the bottom of the wall where the sun shone. Even as she told me the story, my mother's voice betrayed excitement. When her stepmother wasn't looking, she retrieved a small pickle jar from the pantry shelf and hid it under her apron. She stood on a bale of straw, presumably brought to the house to stuff a mattress, leaning over the half-filled rain barrel and reaching down as far as she could. She submerged the pickle jar below the water, insects flicking over the surface and on the dark skin of her arms, including a dragonfly, the sun diamond blue on its wings. Stories warned it would sew your lips together. She retrieved two or three inches of water.

Telling this story, Annie always repeated that it was very important not to let anyone know what she was doing. The best things were always secret, something my mother believed, although unable to express the reasons why. Like the moon, she told me, expecting me to understand the analogy, like the full moon, which she admired through a window when it appeared, it was better to move silently and alone. In the sky she never saw interference with the moon. And if the man in the moon was laughing at her, Annie didn't mind. He certainly didn't listen to her stepmother repeating that she didn't see what was so funny in this world. Stepmother was not known for her sense of humour. So, under the apron went the pickle jar again, secured by one hand as if Annie were holding her belly like the farmers' wives carrying babies inside their bodies.

"Annie, what are you doing?" her stepmother, Tinca, asked without turning around when Annie entered the house again.

"Nothing, Mama."

"You don't have time to do nothing. I need your help."

"Yes, Mama."

But she returned to the children's end of the house, careful not to spill any water, although a few drops slipped out, then upended and pressed the jar against the wall, allowing the water to cover the seedlings. They looked like little green fish with tiny fins under the glass. She did this several times, trying to water as many of the seedlings as she could see before her stepmother noticed and called for help in the kitchen area where she was kneading the dough for *plăcintă*. It was all very well to water the vegetable patch, but to water the bedroom wall! So many years later, and my mother was still astounded by the daring and irrelevance of the action. Water was as precious as the air itself. Wherever she placed the jar, a perfect dark circle appeared on the wall, caused by water seeping into its whitewashed mud.

She slid the pickle jar under the bed, planning to return it to the larder when her stepmother went outside. As the days passed, Annie checked the patch of wall in the corner on the other side of the room, and the green shoots grew bigger and buds formed, and she held her breath from excitement until her lungs forced the air out in soft, whispery explosions. One day several red- and orange-petalled flowers appeared, bursting out of the lower wall. Just like the Indian blanket flowers (gaillardia) growing wild in fields that had not yet been cut open and turned over by harrow and plough. Sometimes weeks went by without rain, and the flowers spread over the land and waved in the wind, thriving in the dry heat of the prairie. Perhaps her flowers on the wall didn't need water to grow. Her parents were so busy in the house and on the farm that they did not notice her garden, and if her sisters who also slept in this room saw the flowers, they said nothing. During the day, they played or worked in the kitchen or outside. No one was allowed to play on the beds once

Tinca had straightened the sheets and covered the two beds with the quilts. At night, the room was dark, lit only by the weak light of the moon and stars in the window, or by one kerosene lamp, which their father snuffed out after the children had said their prayers and climbed onto their straw-filled mattress.

Then on the fourth day of blooming, Annie discovered their heads snapped off and crushed on the floor, the stems and leaves limp along the wall like dead green worms. So, something sudden and beautiful like blanket flowers sprouting on the wall could perish behind her back. She didn't cry. After all, one shouldn't cry over a flower. She didn't know who was responsible.

Let this be a lesson, my mother always said when she told me this story, talking more to herself than to me. Interference: if she didn't take care to guard her actions and thoughts, sooner or later the Devil would flash out of the fiery pits of hell and crush them like the devastated flower heads.

Of all necessary things for the welfare of a Romanian baby, it is imperative that she be received into the Orthodox Church by the threefold immersion of the baptism ritual. The church became an important centre of Annie's consciousness as she grew up, therein seeking explanation and solace, and therefrom fleeing when she deemed it had failed. The church in Dysart was erected out of wood in 1906 and completed in 1907 at the remarkably low cost of $2,400 by Romanian immigrants, her uncle being one of them. The front of St. George Romanian Orthodox Church, now a Canadian heritage site, does not at first remind one of the European Orthodox basilicas. For one thing, the roof of the original building is pitched, not domed. The exterior walls are white board with a centre tower rising to a peak above the entrance.

From certain angles today the church looks distinctly Protestant in its simplicity, although the Catholic church of the community is almost identical, if only because both were designed by the same carpenter-cum-architect. A simple wooden rectangle with five windows on either side, it does not look obviously Byzantine in character from the front until one notices the back, where two circular wings, each topped with a smaller tower, were added on either side of the main building in 1945. The crosses on the tower are of course Byzantine in design. When Annie was baptized there, the church was smaller than it is today, and there were no pews in which to sit, standing in church being the Orthodox tradition. And one can stand a very long time indeed. Modernity or impatience, perhaps the same thing, arthritis and other ailments afflicting the aging devout, led the congregation to install pews at the time of the 1945 renovations.

Step inside and the world of the prairies funnels into a Romanian village *biserică*. There's no mistaking the Byzantine Orthodoxy. The interior walls are panelled wood, and the wood of the ceiling has been adroitly shaped and curved to suggest a dome. The two additional wings are side chapels, and the wooden iconostasis screening the altar, as its name implies, is covered with icons, images of saints, Christ and the Holy Mother of God. The iconostasis can be as rich or modest as money and art allow. Annie was baptized on the eleventh of May under her Romanian name, Ana, in the presence of her parents and her godparents. It would have been inconceivable of them to eschew baptism altogether, a refusal tantamount to damning their child to hell. However incomplete was the church's protection against the Devil, one was entirely at his mercy without the sacrament of baptism. According to Orthodox theory, baptism begins the life of the child in the Church and Christianity, a kind of initiation into the sacrosanct. Immediately after the baptismal ritual, the Sacrament of *Christmation* is performed, a sacrament that confirms (*Christmation* means "confirmation in the Church") and seals God's gifts to the new child. This was certainly incomprehensible to the infant, and understood more sensuously than rationally by Rahila or Samson, who followed ancient practice and, perhaps, enacted undying hope for their daughter.

The Orthodox Church is redolent with incense, the fuming censer dangled from gold chains and swung at various intervals during a service. One inhales the odours of the Holy Ghost. The iconic imagery of a Romanian *biserică* reveals the history of God in heaven and on earth, a text in pictures, a constant reminder of the presence of the sacred in the most mundane lives. In a sense, the baby received the gifts (spiritual rather than material) conveyed by the Holy Spirit. The baptism and confirmation having been followed by Communion, the newborn Ana Corches was fully entered into and became a participant in the centuries-old Byzantine Church. The officiating priest was the Reverend Ghenadie Gheorghiu. Outside, the prairie sky held not so much as a whisper of the Emperor Justinian or Saint Michael or Vlad the Impaler, but inside the church, the baby, wrapped in white shawls specially knitted for the occasion, was safe beneath the hard glittering eyes of the heavily sainted iconostasis.

CHAPTER 2

He who would learn to pray,
let him go to sea.

It was one thing for Annie's parents to leave the land of their ancestors, quite another to vacate the grounds of their mythology and psyche. Both her father, Samson, and her mother, Rahila, devout Orthodox Christians that they were, did not abandon their religious beliefs, cultural attitudes and genetically ingrained superstitions when they boarded ship. Thanks to Bram Stoker and the movies, the non-Romanian world knows about garlic hung from the window or around the neck to ward off vampires—the least of my grandparents' anxieties, although they understood the medicinal and supernatural powers of garlic as well as the next farmer. Prince Vlad Tepes's castle remains standing in Sighisoara. The current Romanian government has announced plans to build a Dracula theme park for tourists in the region, some distance from Samson's birthplace in Cimpina and Rahila's native town of Turda in the Transylvania region of Romania.

More primitive than modern, their minds formed by religious Orthodoxy and an elaborate Church ritual with roots in the Byzantine empire and folklore extending too far back to record, Romanian immigrants left a land tramped upon and governed by ancient Romans, invaded by Turks, later threatened by Russians. From one point of view, Vlad Tepes, the historical prototype for Dracula, was a kind of national hero of Wallachia, an area now incorporated into modern Romania, for defeating and keeping the Turks at bay. Religious jubilation over the victory was great. If Vlad impaled the Turks on sharpened tree trunks, no one then who was not a Turk complained. But people who told Dracula stories (in Romanian, *drac* means "devil"—*du-te dracului* means "go to hell," *la dracu* "damn!"—and the word is also associated with another demonic creature, the dragon) would have to make an enormous intellectual and spiritual adjustment to life on the Canadian prairies. Even today they are not suitable breeding grounds for stories of vampires and the Devil. A landscape of wolf-haunted forests, mountains misty in the distance, a history of bloodthirsty invasions, political instability and slaughters, a Church that encouraged a sensuous and mystical apprehension of the Deity and a subterranean belief in the machinations of the Devil would seem to be requirements. Although castles in one state of disrepair or another dot the hilly, forested landscape, Samson was preoccupied less with blood-sucking vampires, more a Western fascination than a Romanian, than with the momentous transformation of his life.

Posters were plastered over village walls and immigrant agents spread the good word, not to mention whatever letter reached Samson from his brother Simeon, in Canada since 1902. The propaganda machine seduced his imagination. Blood enters the story. In a century of unspeakable slaughters, Romanians contributed their share, both as perpetrators and as victims. Beginning in the first decade, one can't walk very long into the history of twentieth-century Europe without tripping over corpses. My mother yearned to visit Romania, a land that existed in her mind as a kind of magical kingdom. I think the yearning originated in an almost crippling sense of loss rather than a mere desire to travel. By returning to the land whence her parents came, she may have been harbouring a strange, undefined belief in reunification with her beloved father and by now mythical mother. Her parents did not live long enough for Annie to cast a critical eye over them, but long enough to become icons of perfect love and protection after their deaths. One recalls the importance of stylized imagery on icons and the place they hold in Orthodox worship. From the outside iconography looks like mere idolatry: it's not. The icons present an image that reflects and symbolizes divine love, essence and grace. Still, it helps to see what one cannot touch. Even peasants knew they weren't worshipping painted slabs of wood. Annie never saw her parents as Canadians, always as Romanians. She herself spoke more Romanian than English, except to her youngest son. I have heard it said that her Romanian was both fluent and musical; angels would weep to hear. A peculiar allusion. Why would angels cry over wonderful speech? In any case, when means and opportunity allowed, Annie found reasons not to travel to the ancestral homeland. Here, she revealed a deeply rooted sense of realism that probably warned her in some unconscious way against travelling toward a fantasy. Like most people, me included, she knew little of the history of Romania, least of all anything about uprisings and pogroms.

The recent peasant uprising, quelled by government-sanctioned slaughters, and his thirst for land he could call his own without being ruined by taxation, persuaded, then convinced, Samson that it was time to leave. The posters, some little more than handbills promising 160 acres of free property out of the 400 million of arable land available, all written in the local language, constantly reminded Samson that on the other side of the world peace and prosperity were to be found. But to journey to the other side of the world! Harnessed to a plough, trudging through the furrows behind his oxen, he knew the boundaries of his world and, quasi-slavery and taxation and occasional massacres notwithstanding, he lived on familiar terrain. At least Simeon had reached the land of promise and lived to tell the tale, leaving out some of the more disheartening events like prairie fires that swept over the roof of his sod hut.

One Canadian poster portrays a metaphoric lady of the wheat fields, poetically holding a sheaf, the landscape of plenty stretching forever behind her dreamy face. Another announces that "The Last Best West" provided "HOMES FOR MILLIONS." This heart-gripping notion of home reaches deep into the soul and assumes many shapes. Although Samson and Rahila farmed land with little more than hand tools and shepherded flocks of sheep and goats that did not truly belong to them, they derived their sense of purpose from the land they worked. They lived in fabled Transylvania, not so far from the beautiful medieval city of Cluj. The territory shifted political hands so often that citizenship became more a matter of mythology than certainty. And for Romania throughout the centuries, Transylvania had acquired the nature of spiritual necessity, the geographic expression of the very soul of the always emerging, always troubled, nation. Forests and mountains, rivers and hills, fables and folklore, wolves and winds: they were rooted to this place as deeply as the Carpathians and the Transylvanian Alps. To step foot off ancestral territory wrenched the soul.

What, then, was home if what they had loved all their lives, suffering under God's mysterious purpose for the faithful, could no longer shelter and protect them? How was it possible to leave home, to find another? Home was more than the wooden thatch-roofed cottage with the carved porch pillars. It was more than the many wall hangings woven out of red- and blue-dyed yarns and threads, covered with geometric patterns, stylized flowers and birds of folklore like the brilliantly feathered *maiastra*, or the many pots and dishes with cobalt blue designs on the wall rack surrounding the central room. No matter how often used, not even the *spălătoara*, Rahila's washtub on wooden legs, defined home. What choices could Rahila have made among the household goods? They could not pack everything. What dish (*veselă*), which feather-stuffed pillow (*pernă*) in its elaborately embroidered case, what shirt and apron, all covered with intricate stitchery? What blanket (*cuvertură*), some so wonderfully and colourfully woven that they draped the whitewashed walls like tapestries? They could only carry so much.

Surely they could not leave behind the *vârtelniţă*, the spinning wheel at which she had sat dreaming for hours at a time. Samson could not cart the *plug* (plough) or *seceră* (scythe), the animals so necessary to their well-being—*oaie, capră, porc* and *gîscă* (sheep, goat, pig and goose)—clear across the world. He had already chosen which white shirt (*cămaşă*) that she had embroidered, which vest (*vestă*), lambskin jerkin, white wool trousers, his one pair of boots (*lustragiu*) and his wool-lined hat, not the fur cap with the peacock feather. His brother had written not to bring the farm tools, not even the hoe (*sapă*), for they were available in the new land. Leaving behind one's tools and clothes, pots and pans, why, it was abandoning a part of themselves. They would be incomplete human beings. Bright patterns and textures are inextricably woven into the Romanian psyche, something Annie absorbed so effortlessly that she could never explain how she discovered her love of the red rose or why embroidery and crocheting became such an important activity in her life, so fine and convoluted the threads and patterns that she went half-blind over the hooks, threads and needles.

How could either Rahila or Samson choose among the icons, the unchanging, comforting gaze of saints painted on wood or glass? They had to turn their backs on some holy figures. Would

God forgive? How was it possible for their first-born child, Niculai, a hardy boy of three, and their daughter Tenka, born in April of this year, to grow up where the *biserică* did not stand? Without a house, did God survive in the empty land? And what stories would emerge from a place without the darkness of the forests and the mists of the mountains? They would have to remind their children, born and unborn, of the depths of Transylvanian dramas and narratives passed down through the centuries.

One left the physical home only under compelling circumstances, the experience of thousands, including his own brother, testimony to the dictates of history. If paradise beckoned at the end of an unimaginable journey, what devil had so despoiled their home that they were forced to leave? Neither adventurers nor travellers, they saw little reason for wandering the globe, their horizons blocked by the blue-tinged mountains. The body shifted ground, the heart and soul remained. When they selected the icons of the saints Gheorghe and Elisabeta and wrapped them in Rahila's embroidered kerchief, slipped them between the two blankets she had packed in the wooden trunk, their own tears made the saints look as if they were crying. Simeon had written—the village priest had read them the letter—about building his first sod house cut out of that land, Canada, so far away that Samson and Rahila wondered if God would find them. A house of mud without carved and decorated pillars to hold up the roof. Were they swine wallowing in mud? Unafraid of physical labour, for no one worked harder, they believed the purpose of life was not to labour but to enjoy the fruits of labour, work just long enough to maintain the body with time left over to celebrate life. Pigs did not play the pan pipe or dance the *horă* or attend Easter services in the *biserică*. They could not help wondering if constructing a new house in a new land bereft of forest and mountain, a house without carved woodwork, without even a porch, would really replace the home they had always known. Surely a house of mud was a house of unremitting labour. What time for the spirit to dance?

By train, departing from the thirteenth-century city of Cluj, they trundled across continental Europe until they reached Antwerp, their embarkation point for Canada. Their ship was the SS *Montfort* of the Canadian Pacific line. Launched in 1899, it had served as a transport ship in the Boer War. After the European continent, the Atlantic Ocean separates Transylvania from Canada not only in space but also in eons of time. When twenty-nine-year-old Samson Corches boarded ship with his twenty-four-year-old wife, Rahila, and his two children, he was stepping off the edge of his known world to fall into a universe of dreams or devils. How could he know for certain? Unfamiliar with the sea and sailing craft, Rahila and Samson boarded with their two infants, and swallowed their fears as thick in their throats as lumps of *mămăligă*, lugging their trunk and wooden crate and cloth satchels up the gangway to the deck of the 445-foot-long, four-masted, single-stack boat. Their quarters were the steerage, so they descended to the bowels of the boat.

Although surrounded by the walls of the ship's hull, the noise of the engines constant in their ears like the churning of a distant earthquake, they could well have remembered the Romanian story about the Devil who tried to board Noah's ark. The animals trudged and clambered, flew and crept, stomped and scurried two by two up the plank. The Devil disguised himself as one of the creatures threatened with extinction. Fortunately adept at mathematics, Noah discovered the ruse by counting and excluding the third cat or whatever other animal shape, depending upon variants, the Devil assumed. This story can be understood as a testament to the Devil's devious trickery, or God's ultimate purpose, which did not allow for the presence of evil on the boat, or human organizational genius in the face of catastrophe. It's a wonderful example of the Romanian belief that goodness, like a ship at sea, rocks and rolls and sometimes founders and sinks, that all the prayers in the world may offer solace but no guarantees. And, perhaps like Noah, Rahila and Samson were sore afraid. For God had promised, "I will bring a flood of waters upon the earth, to destroy all flesh in which is the breath of life from under heaven." What security lay beneath their feet when the land itself had disappeared, what help for them if the waters broke through the hull and drowned them all? The first and last time in their life on board a ship, they unwrapped their icons and kissed the relentlessly austere faces of the saints.

So many photographs and movies we have seen over the years of Eastern Europeans crowded on steamships and trains, clustered among their baggage and children on the docks, thousands of miles from their places of origin: and the images convey little of what went on in their minds. Closer to the past in their perceptions than the present, how the sea voyage must have wrenched their nervous systems and sense of reality. Before the invention of the airplane, a fear of water substituted for a fear of flying. Not everyone readily took to the sea, least of all an ignorant peasant accustomed to the density and certainty of the land. A good man is steady behind the plough, a woman knows where she is planting seeds in the furrow. God watches over us and the Devil lays his snares, but we know where we are. Staring over the railing at the grey or blue of limitless waves, sky without end, no landmark, no solid ground, no familiar mountain (*munte*) in the distance, constant movement, their minds filled with stories of travellers who never returned and never arrived, between singing and chatting about families left behind and the Canadian government's promise of land, eating cold week-old *mămăligă*, many Romanians prayed daily.

Consider medieval cartography and all the monsters of the deep swimming on the edges of the maps or sometimes poking their carnivorous maws above the main to frighten sailors. We don't paint pictures of our fears in the sky, but some of us imagine fearful scenarios when we fly. In his sheepskin pouch, Samson carried an icon of *Sfântu* Gheorghe. At night Rahila's uneasy mind, overwhelmed by the inexplicable immensity of the starry sky, found confirmation of God's existence, like Jane Eyre on the moor enthralled by the Milky Way. As the ship sidled and rocked, Rahila, already the mother of two children, believed paradoxically that however universal evil was, geographic restrictions applied. In the midst of her hope and mind-gnawing worry, she remembered that the Devil, unaided, supposedly could not cross the water.

Another Romanian creation myth depicts God chatting with the Devil, both equal powers, both sharing primordial substance. They are sitting on a wave. God requests that the Devil dive to the bottom of the pre-existent sea for a handful of clay or slime or a combination of both. Always the gentleman, the Devil complies, dives, scoops and resurfaces, primordial mud in hand. God then fashions himself a spot of dry land where He can rest without getting soaked. And the Omnipotent one falls asleep. Jealousy over God's ingenuity and creation infects the Devil's spirit, his change in demeanour unaccountable except it must lie in his primordial nature to go bad sooner or later. Seeing his advantage over the slumberous God, Satan tries to push God into the sea, where He will drown.

The interesting implication here is that God, aside from being unable to swim, is not by nature omnipotent or omniscient. One can see why the Church needed to act quickly in this matter. He is, however, a superior wrestler and forces the Devil back, each move extending the patch of land. Through the struggle between Good and Evil, the world emerges. But the land stretches so far and wide that the sky is too limited to cover it. An imperfect architect, God seeks advice from the hedgehog and the birds to make everything fit. To the victor goes the land, something the Native peoples of Canada discovered to their detriment in the nineteenth century. Pushed off the world, the Devil has no choice but to retreat underground, where he forges his demonic realm and causes problems for the peasants. He also loses his fondness for water.

In Samson's case, anxiety over the future was eased by more than a simple belief in God's great goodness. A tangible guarantee waited at the other end of the voyage. He was not sailing into unknown seas so much as following his oldest brother. Would the patron saint of Romania extend his beneficent powers over the waves? From the deck of the ship in the Antwerp port, he could see the Gothic spire of Our Lady's Cathedral, the highest structure in the city. Although Catholic and not Orthodox, the one and only true faith, as the priests so often reminded them, the visible church persuaded Samson that he and his family had not yet fallen off the edge of the world. The tower confirmed God's presence.

Yet, in a world where one week they had trudged the furrows of terra firma and the next week rocked on the waters, what assurances could be found once they sailed out of sight of God's house? Lord have mercy. Seeking comfort, Samson repeated like a response in the church that his brother had gone before, as had many thousands of others, and survived. So he held little Niculai in his arms as Rahila suckled the baby, and their dark eyes stared out in the shadows of the steerage at the other immigrants, also separated from everything they knew and hoping to reach paradise as well.

The *Montfort* sailed from Antwerp on October 27, 1909. There were 306 passengers aboard this particular journey, almost all of them steerage. Aside from the Corches family, families from Austria and Russia and Poland also tried to be comfortable and to quell their anxieties. The ship arrived at Quebec City on November 7, docking at 13:05 p.m. The ship's surgeon had to certify that he had "made a general inspection of the passengers on this vessel," and had "seen no passenger thereon who . . . is, or is likely to become, insane, epileptic or consumptive, or who is idiotic, feeble-minded or afflicted with a contagious, infectious or loathsome disease; or who is deaf, dumb or blind or otherwise physically defective or whose present appearance would lead [him] to believe that he or she might be debarred from entering Canada." It's reassuring to know that one's ancestors passed official muster, but how the medical examiner, who was not a polyglot and relied on translators and guesswork, determined feeble-mindedness or the likelihood of maintaining sanity is difficult to gauge.

A family legend exists about a relative, a young girl, who died at sea. My mother repeated the story, sometimes confusing her family's immigrant experience with that of her husband's, until one sometimes lost track in her later life of whom she was speaking. Whether the story is true or not matters less than the fact that my mother had incorporated it into her own mythology of her past. A young, of course beautiful, girl, dying on the ocean on her way to a better life. Annie shook her head as if to say, What did one expect? How she absorbed that story as a reflection of herself reveals a deep sense of a life unlived, identifying as she did with a woman of whom she knew nothing, who apparently had perished at sea even before her life had begun. Immigrants did die at sea, but a Corches was not among them. More likely than death on board was the occurrence of conjunctivitis, sometimes cholera or typhus. Some immigrants perished from these diseases, more in the nineteenth century than the twentieth, living quarters being dark, stuffy, damp and crowded, water supply and sanitary conditions less than ideal. By the time Samson and Rahila boarded ship with their children, conditions had improved.

An extraordinary sense of dislocation and otherworldliness gripped their hearts as they rocked in the steerage, or caught a breath of air on deck, a relief from the putrid odours of feces and urine and unwashed bodies, only superficially suppressed by the stench of disinfectant below deck. There was no way to bathe during the two-week crossing. Men and women separated on either side of the steerage passageway, families together, everyone essentially incomprehensible, privacy virtually impossible, they slept with their clothes on, removing at most one layer. How difficult to keep the children quiet, to hear one's own prayers in the night. Could His eyes penetrate to the bottom of the boat and protect the terrified and helpless faithful?

If the seas were not too rough on a rainy day, they watched the sky and ocean merge, distinctions disappearing in relentless grey. During high seas, they were compelled to remain below deck, the locking of the hatches reminding them of what little freedom they could exercise. On the ocean, bereft of markers, they could not really see where they were or where they were going, trusting in the ship's captain, who did not speak their language, and in Simeon's letter, which they carried with them as a talisman, more powerful than the cross. In a world where God seemed to have disappeared, safety and solidity existed at the end of the journey. As they had prayed in the Cimpina church before they and other wayfarers trundled in carts for the train in Cluj, they both searched their souls, hoping, as their hands turned white on the rails and they stared out to sea, that they had not invited the Devil to travel with them. *Aduci pe dracul în casă cu lautări si apoi nu-l scoti cu o mie de popi*: he that takes the Devil into his boat must carry him over the sound. Rahila had no choice but to depend on the strength of her husband, not really recognizing her own courage and stamina. Her black hair covered with a *basma* (kerchief) patterned with birds and flowers, black prayer beads twisted among her stubby fingers, the baby wrapped in a shawl and pressed against her breasts, she whispered the priest's prayer in the *biserică* from *Ectenia Mică*, the Little Litany: *Apară, mântuieşte, miluieşte şi ne păzeşte pe noi, Dumnezeule cu harul Tău.* Help and save us, have mercy on us and keep us, O God, by your grace. Samson, little Niculai by his side, hearing Rahila pray in the wind, repeated the cantor's response to the priest: *Doamne miluieş te.* Lord have mercy.

Mercy being granted, the ship sailed into the English Channel, south past Dover and Plymouth, England, and west across the Atlantic, passing the Scilly islands off the tip of Cornwall, and reached the Quebec City docks without incident. The *Montfort* would make many such voyages until it was commandeered to carry supplies during the First World War. Mercy being finite and the ship ending its days as it began as a miliary transport, the *Montfort* was torpedoed by a German U-boat on October 1, 1918, southwest of Bishop's Rock, Scilly Isles. Five people lost their lives. Lord have mercy.

CHAPTER 3

*It is good to light a candle
to the Devil also every now and then.*

Trains always captured Annie's imagination. Train tracks played a major role in her fantasies, and for most of her life, certainly throughout my childhood, she lived close enough to trains to feel the rented homes shake and creak as the cars rumbled along their tracks. On one level, proximity to trains is no more than historical necessity, as even a superficial knowledge of prairie towns can testify; on another, the harsh fact of poverty determined residence in her later life, as trains tend to cut through poor sections of town. But on the deepest level that goes beyond transportation and economics, beyond her resentment of poverty and inconvenient dwellings, the train reminded Annie of her childhood fantasies and frustrations. What used to be the quintessentially collective Canadian experience of the transcontinental train became for Annie an individual metaphor of yearning and despair. It was fitting that her parents, like thousands of other immigrants, should have depended on the CPR to reach their final destination in Saskatchewan, although they had little idea what the journey across thousands of miles of tracks entailed, once they disembarked at Quebec City.

Northrop Frye has written that the difference between reaching Canada and the United States by ship is that the possibility of seeing land and still sailing on exists for immigrants to Canada in the way it does not for those headed for the States. Spotting land in the distance, travellers to Canada are not directly confronted with a seacoast and can enter unknown waters because the Gulf of St. Lawrence and the river itself beckon the ship, waters that ultimately lead to the belly of the continent. Out of that geographic peculiarity, much metaphor can be made. As the *Montfort* sailed into Canadian waters, Newfoundland to the north, Prince Edward Island and Nova Scotia to the south, Samson and Rahila may well have felt, metaphorically speaking, what Frye postulated. Emerging from their own ship's belly, their skin grey with grime, their clothes musty, their minds dazed and befuddled by two weeks in steerage, their heads still buzzing from the babel of languages in the steerage, they said a prayer to express their relief, attributing to God what the ship's captain and crew had achieved. The peasant instinct was to thank the Lord for the normal course of events and to blame the Devil for everything else. My mother did as much, until she stopped thanking God altogether.

Approaching the Quebec City docks on November 7, 1909, Rahila and Samson looked up to the top of Cap Diamant and saw the Château Frontenac, little more than twenty years old at the time, standing like the castle of a Romanian boyar in the Carpathians. What comfort they derived from that is a matter of supposition, but after two weeks on the ocean, rock and building were assuredly welcome sights. Free from contagion, not even afflicted with conjunctivitis, the scourge of steerage, able to respond to questions through a translator, once they dragged themselves and their possessions down the gangplank, the immigrants underwent due process, their physical and mental health guaranteed by the medical examiners, Drs. Nadeau and Dobbin, a process that took surprisingly little time when one considers the doctor had to sign a warranty against lunacy. Only four immigrants who had sailed on the *Montfort* were detained. The examination completed at 2:35 p.m, Annie's parents were taken to the railway station and left by special train at four o'clock, less than three hours after docking.

On the wooden seats of the immigrant train car warmed by a Quebec heater, they passed days and nights that seemed to stretch as long as the interminable miles of track, and rumbled across the Quebec, Ontario, Manitoba landscapes, each mile working deep into their consciousness of distance, separation and, above all, nervous expectation. At the end of the line, according to promise, a familiar face would eventually greet them. Samson's brother Simeon had not been swallowed by monsters of the deep, a fact repeated like a prayer.

With the soporific rhythm of the rocking train, Rahila sang lullabies to her restless children, secured the red ribbon around baby Tenka's wrist to ward off the evil eye (*deochi*) and fed them what food was available, not only to ease their discomfort but to quell the terror in her heart. Never having prepared for a journey before, least of all one that took more than two weeks, she had not packed enough food. On the boat they had consumed all the *mămăligă*, four heavy cakes of it, each one weighing two pounds, the cured pork hocks, the rye bread that had turned mouldy within days on the sea, the cheese *plăcintă*, and had to rely on the ship's distribution of food for the rest of the journey. Her own parents, kissing her goodbye before their daughter's departure for Cluj, food packed in crates, were also undertaking the momentous journey on another ship to the new land. What guarantees existed that they would ever see one another again? To Romanians, family is all-important, and the wrenching apart of hers, the previously unimaginable distance between her children and their grandparents, an abstraction rendered visible outside the window as the train chugged along the shores of Lake

Superior, past forests and lakes and rocks and marshes reminiscent of Transylvania, bespoke loss and regret.

The peasant mind is difficult to fathom, but where there is mind, there is imagination. Centuries of Romanian stories and images and folk knowledge account for the contradictions of life, misery and ill fortune, and everything that cannot be understood. Martyrs and demons, pigsties and sheep, brilliantly coloured threads woven into mythical birds and flowers, geometric patterns in red and cobalt blue, the evil eye winking from dark corners—all passed through Rahila's mind as quickly as the train rumbled past the trees of the north Superior shore. Falling asleep, waking up, dreaming in hope and despair, she prayed. God is great, of course He is, but a wise woman wards off the evil eye and knows that Satan can hide in a pile of stones. If Samson sat on the edge of his seat, his cap on his knees, his eyes darting with fear and anticipation, she tried her best to thank God for safe delivery and not to cloud her mind with memories of the pots and pans, blankets and tapestries, and her parents who, at this very moment, could be sinking beneath the ocean waves. The movements of her arm restricted by the three blouses she wore under her coat and shawls, she crossed herself in the Orthodox fashion. So much left behind.

Uncertainty lay ahead. In Transylvania, however hard life was, uprisings and pogroms bloodying the landscape at times, she knew where she was. Constant movement for the past few weeks, the air of the passenger car fetid from pipe smoke and the fug created by the Quebec heater, and forests and rocks giving way to the seemingly flat Manitoba terrain, eradicated her sense of place. Not even the train from Cluj across Europe had instilled such anxiety; at least she recognized the beginning of her journey there, heard her own language, and even if they got off the train in a foreign city whose name she had never heard before, she, too, had recognized a human city and a holy church and people very much like herself. And Rahila stared at her reflection in the nighttime glass of the train window, seeing the terror in her dark eyes. Within four years Rahila would die. Of this she would have no premonition.

It's a fanciful notion to believe that children absorb characteristics from their mother's milk, when personal and historical circumstances provide more plausible reasons, but departures and separations, each riddled with sorrow and anxiety, became such a regular feature of Annie's young life that she lost all faith in human relationships, even as she strove to fulfill the demands of her heart. Her parents left a geography, not a way of viewing the world. Although they emigrated from Romania, they carried their culture in their speech, song, dance and understanding. The "foreignness" in the deepest sense of these people, their primitive qualities as perceived by Canadian sophisticates of English and French extraction, aroused fury in some quarters. Although encouraged to come to Canada by means of an effective propaganda campaign in the old country, they were regarded as little better than oxen capable of dragging a plough. Clifford Sifton's famous definition of the kind of immigrants he was looking for as minister of the interior bears repeating:

> When I speak of quality I have in mind something that is quite different from what is in the mind of the average writer or speaker upon the question of immigration. I think that a stalwart peasant in a sheepskin coat, born to the soil, whose forefathers have been farmers for ten generations, with a stout wife and half-dozen children, is good quality.

I suppose this is a statement of high praise if one ignores the implicit animal metaphor. Forward-looking Sifton also seems to be congratulating himself on his above-average perception. The "average writer or speaker on the question of immigration" might have had something like the following in mind:

> What Sifton means by affecting not to know that there is such a place as Great Britain on the map, and ignoring Britishers as desirable immigrants, preferring to minister with the power behind him and the funds at his disposal to the importing of a mass of human ignorance, filth and immorality is only known to his immediate friends, Silver-tongued Wilf [Wilfrid Laurier], Yukon Bill, and other dubious characters.

How did this blistering denunciation that appeared on January 18, 1899, in the *Calgary Herald* apply to poor Rahila Corches? A young Romanian mother of two children, nauseated on the boat from seasickness, anxiety and terror, doing no more than faithfully adhering to the laws of matrimony according to the rites of her Church, was filthy for the duration of the crossing. On the farm in Romania, Rahila had trudged in cow flaps and dug her fingers deep into the soil, but left her boots outside and washed her hands in a pail before entering her home. Inside, she scoured not only table and floors but also her body. Cleanliness was not exclusively a Puritan preoccupation. The Romanians, dare I say, were as clean as the English.

Ignorance, however, is an honest charge, more difficult to dispute. Rahila was illiterate. Schooling, if available for Romanian peasant girls, would have been severely restricted. Her knowledge of the greater world was perhaps not equal to that of the many thousands of lower-class, semi-literate British immigrants who also crossed the ocean and had no more opportunity for washing than Romanians or Bulgarians or Russians. What perverse fantasies and stereotypes resided in the mind of the editorialist is impossible to say, but the charge of immorality, so irrelevant as to be risible, could only have originated in a psychotic dream or a bizarre notion of Balkan sexuality. Was Rahila a whore? Samson a rake and brothel keeper? Were Canadian children safe? Had the editorialist read stories of the psychopathic Countess Bathory? She was Hungarian, in any case, but virulence often overlooks cultural distinctions.

On a more urbane level, the influx of Eastern European immigrants raised the romantic idealization and mockery of Stephen Leacock. Twelve years later in an article entitled "Canada and the Immigration Problem," Leacock, an anglophile and writer of mildly humorous satires, pontificates as well as any:

> Still more important is the economic and racial character of the immigrants of the twentieth century. They no longer consist of the strenuous, the adventurous, the enterprising; they are not, except in a minor degree, political exiles or religious refugees; they are animated by no desire to build up a commonwealth of freedom to replace an ungrateful fatherland. They are, in great measure, mere herds of the proletariat of Europe, the lowest classes of industrial society, without home and work, fit objects indeed for philanthropic pity, but indifferent material from which to build the commonwealth of the future.

Confusing bigotry with knowledge, Leacock betrays, aside from prejudice, an ignorance of history and human motive. My favourite Leacock sneer in the same speech, unintentionally funny (perhaps not) is a later reference to "ethnological curiosities." As a descendent of freaks, I can only say "ouch." Sticks and stones may break our bones, but we're naive if we think names don't hurt. Given the sheer volume of immigrants, the protests are little more than fingers in the proverbial dike, understandable reactions in the wake of change. On the francophone side, Henri Bourassa foams at the mouth, lamenting in a parliamentary speech that it is "a providential condition of our partly French and partly English country to make it a land of refuge for the scum of all nations." Although these are individual men, the official voice often speaks for many. One assumes an audience sympathetic to the rhetoric. Happy to say, Samson and Rahila, comforting their children and each other on board ship, were completely oblivious to the venom spat at them from the polished, distinctly xenophobic sidelines.

Born and raised in the New World, Annie had her perceptions shaped, perhaps distorted, by elements of the Old. A dark strain, call it fatalism or superstition, compromised my mother's understanding of life. Whatever was good always seemed more illusory than real, happiness, however richly felt at the time, just momentary respite from sorrow. Her desire for solid ground, a place she could say she truly possessed, remained with her until the end of her life.

When she finally owned a house, she did not feel entirely comfortable within its walls, shifting on her chairs and constantly finding chores to keep her moving, restless as a pacing panther in a cage. Bitterest irony of all for the child of Romanian peasants and a woman who craved the security of a fixed place, she did not die in her own house. Like her mother on the train, Annie lived in a state of dispossession and yearning. So whenever a train passed by, starting from somewhere Annie had not been and travelling toward a place she would rather be, she would slip into a private dream in the kitchen as the walls of the house shook, soup ladle poised over the steaming pot or flour dough sticking to her fingers.

The train carrying her parents, though, did eventually stop in Regina, where the many hundreds of immigrants, identified by the officials, were given directions through interpreters at the immigration centre on St. John Street. Not far down the road stood, and still stands in renovated form, St. Nicholas, the first Romanian Orthodox church in Canada, indeed, in North America, erected in 1902. This fact is significant. Romanians first arrived in Saskatchewan in the 1890s. In 1902, 152 Romanians were admitted to Canada, among them Samson's brother. In 1909 the Corches family were among the 307 Romanian immigrants, a number that exceeded 1,500 in 1913. As officials, mostly Anglo-Saxon, sometimes confused Romanians with Hungarians or other minorities of the Austro-Hungarian Empire, the numbers may not be entirely accurate. The onset of the First World War, of course, altered travel plans.

The construction of a church by so few, therefore, so far from their homeland, testifies to the central importance of the Church to the Romanian sense of identity. My mother maintained a healthy skepticism about priests and Church doctrines insofar as she understood them. "The nearer the Church, the farther from God," she said on more than one occasion. For virtually all Romanians of the community, though, the Church participated in their lives from birth to death. One could even say "defined," except that the physical demands of the land gave as much purpose and definition as the spiritual world of the Church. In Dysart, above the territory of the dispossessed Crees, Assiniboines and Saulteaux, who had no understanding of secular or religious calendars, rose the wooden basilica dedicated to the greater glory of the Orthodox God, named after St. George.

So many days of the Church calendar honour one martyr or another that believers can feast and pray half their life away.

There is something rather bizarre and disorienting about the construction of an essentially Byzantine *biserică*, however humble, on a prairie landscape. As she grew up, Annie developed a contradictory, sometimes hostile, attitude toward the Church to which she had often turned for explanation and solace. None forthcoming, she resented what had not consoled. For several years, she hung an Orthodox crucifix on her bedroom wall, but often took it down and buried it under her girdles in a bureau drawer, returning it to the wall at Easter, the holiest time of the year for Orthodox Christians. In some sense the crucifix acted as a talisman. It was possible protection against further woes. Possible, not guaranteed. Although sometimes going through religious rituals as if she believed in them, my mother eventually ceased to place much trust in heavenly help. In her experience, God had been more arbitrary and negligent than benign and consistent in His regard for the suffering. Nonetheless, she kept the crucifix as a kind of archaeological artifact from her past, a shard of belief that once existed.

Exhaustion bending their bones, their bodies thick with unpleasant odour, their stomachs craving substantial, properly cooked meals, Rahila, Samson and their two children did not have time to attend services and praise God. They had to board another train. The end was now imaginable. If they had indeed travelled to the end of the world, they had not dropped off the edge after all. My mother's habit of pausing in her work and slipping into reverie has a complex origin, but it's related to the peasant tendency to absorb initial shock or to register complex, contradictory impressions and sensations by seemingly stupefied silence. Under the prairie sky that forces the eye heavenward, her parents, burdened by layers of clothes, stood on the platform with their baggage and babies, papers in hand, instructions slipping out of their grasp, waiting for yet another "monster" to swallow them whole and take them to the promised land. Words failed. Samson tried to speak as he hoisted Tenka in his arms and Rahila wiped Niculai's nose. God had delivered them from the belly of the beast at sea, to be sure, and perhaps the Devil stayed behind (but how could one be sure of that?).

Having arrived in late November, they would soon experience their first prairie winter. There was little time to spare. Here they were in a land that was not theirs but to which, by virtue of a piece of paper, they now had entitlement. They had also freed themselves from the shaking and growling of the train. Now, perhaps wiser through experience, they waited for another with less trepidation. Some sense of relief also came to them when a stranger spoke Romanian and interceded on their behalf at the immigration house, and time permitting, it was possible to pray at St. Nicholas. It was always wise to light a candle of thanksgiving, to light a candle for Rahila's parents, also bound for the new land, perhaps for Simeon who, bless him, waited not so far away. Perhaps it would be wise to remind themselves of the evils they had not encountered but that forever lurked in the midst of happiness, waiting to pounce and devour. No time, no time, the translator said—the train would soon depart.

Simeon had promised to meet them at the Dysart station. The origin of Dysart's name, christened by a Scottish CPR engineer after a village in Scotland, is poetically relevant to a woman of my mother's background and character. According to an ancient tale, a hermit, later canonized as Saint Serf, once lived on the premises of a Carmelite monastery in the vicinity of Dysart in Fife, Scotland. The legend describes how he confronted and wrestled with the Devil, locally referred to as "auld Nick." Winning the contest, Saint Serf banished the Devil from the area, keeping it safe henceforward from all demonic trickery and machinations. There is a saying in the Fife region about time and history, "as old as the three trees of Dysart." The Saskatchewan village, set on a prairie landscape of startling, dynamic and often shifting beauty and varied flora, certainly older than the three trees of Dysart, had no trees to shade the streets during Annie's childhood. The first significant trees were planted in 1929. The saplings survived the first winter and thereafter flourished.

North of the Qu'Appelle Valley, Dysart now is a typical prairie village on the wane, home to its citizens, smaller now than it was in the past, containing cultural echoes of its first inhabitants. Although its people are hospitable, a strange kind of melancholy hovers in the air, the sadness that comes from aging and depletion. Although side streets of the pleasant community are heavily treed, the main thoroughfare is remarkably broad like that of most Saskatchewan towns and villages, designed to allow wagons and horses and farm machinery to manoeuvre easily and turn around. The single remaining grain elevator rises, of course, above the train tracks at one end of the main street, now called McKendre.

By horse and wagon, Simeon would cart his brother's family and their possessions over a road—more a path beaten down by wagon wheels than a road—to their section of the promised land marked out by numbered stakes pounded in the ground at the four corners. They would live with him until Samson had cut blocks of sod, fashioned them into a home and ploughed several acres of land to indicate sincerity of purpose and stability. The government allowed three years for the transformation of once-held Cree territory into a European farm. Neither boyars nor slaughtering soldiers would prevent the new life.

CHAPTER 4

A man without a wife is but half a man.

In the same year as Ana's birth, Samson's mother, Elena, died at the age of fifty-eight. My mother knew very little about this woman. My paternal great-grandparents had crossed the ocean ahead of their son Samson and his family, more than likely arriving with his brothers Simeon and Anton, an infant then, at the turn of the century or on a separate ship, the division of families for immigration purposes being a fairly common procedure. The death of a peasant woman is of no great historical moment, but the personal consequences of the death of a mother run deep like underground rivers and streams feeding the prairie sloughs with many tributaries, welling up in the oddest places, seemingly going dry and disappearing, then springing up years later. For a Romanian, as must be true of any people who place primary importance on the family, a mother's death shatters its central core, breaking its life-sustaining heart. Samson was an adult, mature enough to accept and absorb the blow and understand the fact of death, deriving consolation and explanation, if need be, from the Church.

Annie, however, was little more than a year old when her own mother died on September 25, 1914, several weeks after the declaration of war among the European empires. If it had not been sudden, Rahila would have prepared for her death by daily prayers before her favourite icon, possibly a patron saint or the Mother of God. Adding to her regrets and sorrow over leaving her young family, she lay dying separated from her parents, who had also immigrated to the new world but not to any region Rahila could have visited. For reasons that remain obscure, my mother's maternal grandparents eventually found themselves in Montana and many years later would play a significant part in her life. Whether Rahila's children surrounded her on her deathbed, the youngest, Ana, held in her father's arms, we do not know. Similarly, any comment about what she learned at her mother's breast is more suppositional than factual. Like any Romanian mother Rahila at least coddled and sang to the child suckling at her breast and tried her best to feed, clothe and love. At fifteen or sixteen months, a baby knows her mother and has already absorbed more than mother's milk.

The mother of five children in a sod house on newly churned prairie land has little time to spare for the niceties of family feeling, but in a Romanian family, the mother is so inextricably indispensable to the household that the home psychologically and spiritually collapses without her presence. My mother often spoke about taking food out of her own mouth to feed her young, a concept that, however unappetizing, remains lifesaving for the children. Given the number of impoverished years when she struggled to put food on the table, the metaphor expressed real anxiety and self-sacrifice.

Whatever feelings of maternal love and warmth Annie experienced at her mother's breast were suddenly interrupted. Historically, it's common for mothers to die at a remarkably young age. Rahila was only twenty-nine at the time. A child, to paraphrase Hamlet's mother, should not forever look for her mother in the dust. This may be true if the ghost of the parent doesn't haunt the child's life. Many infants who lose their mother grow up without remembering who she was or the subtle and profound connections between child and mother and manage very happily indeed. Others, like Annie, yearn throughout their lives for what they had never possessed. Some motherless children grow up seemingly unaffected by the loss, develop perfectly natural and happy relationships and get on with their lives. My mother remained haunted by the presence of a mother whom she never knew, a fact that enabled her to fancy what her mother must have or could have been. "If only my mother had lived," she began many a sentence. Suppositional thinking is common among the disappointed. In Annie's case, it derived not only from regret over what she never knew but also from the prolonged brutality of later experience.

Samson, still a young and vigorous man in his early thirties, father of five children, often inseparable from the ploughs to which he harnessed himself as horse or oxen trudged through the furrows of the fields, despaired on at least two counts. His beloved Rahila had died for reasons that to this day remain unknown. In the church register, her death is recorded as *"extraordinara."* With no other information available, one may suppose, given the "extraordinary" circumstance, death by accident. Farms are dangerous places. Examine the blades of various ploughs and harrows of the time and imagine tripping over them. If Rahila died in childbirth, a sad but common phenomenon of the time and no surprise to Romanian women who came from a country with the highest infant mortality rate in Europe at the turn of the century, there's no record. Samson's beloved wife, the mother of his children—dead—so young. Grief was great. He walked the newly ploughed prairie field one very cool night, for it was the end of September and the frosts come early in that part of the world, the moon bathing his sod house in white, and sang the famous *"Miorița,"* the Ewe-lamb, a shepherd's *doină* (song), a kind of anthem for the Romanian peasant, sung on many occasions and connected with the peasant's notion of ancestry, his direct knowledge of life and death, and his apprehension of spiritual power.

Overcoming the debilitating effects of grief as quickly as possible, for the land was unkind to the inattentive, Samson still risked falling into despair over a second, potentially more enduring, cause. How was it possible to raise farm buildings and five children; tend to flocks and small herds and five children, ages eight, four, three, two and one; plough, seed and harvest 160 acres, and clothe and feed five very young children without a helpmate? What does a man do with babies and children when most of his time must be spent out of doors? In her short lifespan as an adult woman Rahila had borne several children with every expectation of living to see them reach adulthood, marry and have children of their own. She had been so strong and healthy. Children not only provided necessary help on the farm, but also guaranteed a man's importance in the eyes of his community, fulfilled God's commandment to be fruitful and multiply and conferred a kind of immortality on the most anonymous. But diapers had to be boiled. Samson, therefore, required a woman. Love and passion did not play a significant role in his selection of a second wife. Interdependent need determined both his proposal to the woman of his choice and her acceptance. Like royalty, peasants often married for reasons other than romance.

On November 22, 1914, two months after Rahila's burial on September 26, Samson married a widow of thirty-two years of age in the St. George Romanian Orthodox Church of Dysart. The Romanians of the community all knew one another or about one another and they would have met in church. It was possible that a marriage broker arranged to bring the two together in matrimony. In Orthodoxy, matrimony, albeit a blessed union, is not regarded as so holy that it cannot be severed. Tolerant and understanding of human foibles and frailties, the Church allows one to marry and divorce three times without threat of expulsion. If you haven't got it right after three attempts, it's suggested that you go elsewhere for benediction. Divorce, however, in both of Samson's marriages was never an issue.

Annie knew her stepmother as Tinca. Tall and narrow in build, rather angular and severe in appearance, Tinca came to this second marriage with at least one child by her first husband. For the most part, Annie remained silent about her stepmother, although, her brother Nick later said, she was not a "very nice" woman. The implication behind my mother's few words about Tinca is that she was humourless and cold. Contrary to fairy tales and folklore, she wasn't necessarily cruel, threatening to chop up or abandon her stepchildren in the forests. The latter endeavour would have been particularly difficult in a territory where forests in any European folkloric sense of the term did not grow. It's conceivable, given the brief two months of their courtship, that Tinca entered the marriage under psychological stress herself, shy in front of five children who were not her own.

She was a hard worker, and work meant work and not play. If all work and no play meant she risked dullness, quite contrary to the Romanian character, there's little evidence to suggest indifference. She cared for the children's well-being but was in all likelihood extremely hard-pressed for time. The physical cruelty toward my mother would come later from another person, one related by blood. More seriously, Tinca would be unable to fulfill Ana's hunger for maternal love and protection. Her sense of being bereft, which she could not have articulated as an infant, deepened in early childhood.

Annie always spoke fondly of her father, although her memory of him weakened over the years and she romanticized the one parent to compensate for the absence of the other. As a Romanian farmer at the turn of the century, struggling to establish and secure himself, as much shepherd as farmer in the old country, Samson spent only a little time with his children in the capacity of loving and nurturing parent. Raising children was women's work.

From dawn to dusk, Samson wore his boots (*lustragiu*) and lambskin jerkin and would rather swing his *seceră* (scythe) than his children and slop the pigs, when he acquired them, in the *cocină* (sty) than feed the kids. His back aching from the harness with which he attached himself to the *plug* (plough) and the uneven trudge over the furrows, he could spare little energy to frolic with the children. And yet—this is the remarkable detail that gripped Annie's memory all her life—he sang and played the *tilinca*, the shepherd's pipe similar to the recorder, essentially a wooden tube with no holes for fingering. And she remembered once his extraordinary and energetic dancing of the *horă*, the Romanian round dance that is a celebration of existence itself under the eyes of God, on an occasion when the entire community had gathered to celebrate. He also publicly broke into song on the same occasion. That was the only time (tears glistening in her eyes when she told me the tale) her father picked her up. I don't believe it was the only time he had done so but do believe it was the only time Annie remembered his doing so. Although she was just six, Samson's presence and personality were beginning to impress themselves on her understanding and imagination.

She liked to say he was a handsome man, but that too may be more wishful thinking than reality, more the result of a need to idealize her father as someone wonderful to hang on to in a world where most of her youthful relations were cut with swift and merciless severity. It is possible to form an objective view of the matter from photographs of Samson, two of which still exist.

In one he is standing alone, his hand resting on the back of an office chair on which, although only partially present, a baby is clearly being held. A deliberately posed photograph, taken by a travelling photographer who made a living driving from community to community. In the other photograph, Samson appears holding a drink in his left hand at the back of a festive crowd. This photo was taken in the summer of 1919, and the former, given his appearance and the presence of a baby, more than likely one of his two children by Tinca, perhaps a year later.

With no information besides the image, one can easily read character into photographed faces. There in the arch of the eyebrow one sees the man's arrogance, or there in the softness of the cheeks his sentimentality, or there in the weak chin his pusillanimity, or there in the dark eyes his smouldering passion. Much of that, of course, is mere projection of the perceiver's agenda or nonsense or both. From his photographs, one can see very little of Samson's mind and character. Like so many Romanians, he was a man of dark complexion, sporting quite a bold moustache and occasionally a trim beard, of wiry or athletic build, average to tall in height and with a pleasing appearance for a Romanian peasant. As to character, one doesn't need a photograph to believe that Samson was imaginative and courageous enough to visualize a new life on the other side of the world, possessed of enough sense to understand that what he had in Transylvania was considerably less than what he would gain in Canada.

Romanians do not necessarily put work before life, but Samson was a hardy enough worker to build a house and plough the land. Not entirely illiterate like so many peasants, he could sign his own name on government documents and add a brief description of his livestock and farm buildings. He was obviously sensual and sexually interested in and attractive to women, as evidenced by the birth of seven children by two wives in a dozen years. It was not only the need for workers to till the soil or slough the pigs that aroused Samson's ardour.

And there was music in his soul. Annie said so, but he was a Romanian, still very much attached to his ancestry, and he therefore relied on music, on the sounds of the *nai* (pan pipe), *toacă* (bellboard), *tilinca*, and the lyrics of the haunting *doinele* (songs), a language to express what would otherwise have remained forever silenced. My mother also said that she didn't remember Samson's ever beating her. Having experienced what that could mean, she perhaps loved her father all the more in retrospect because he never raised a fist or swung a belt against his child.

If childhood can be paradise, Annie's early childhood, in spite of the death of her mother, a somewhat distant stepmother and the hunger in her heart for maternal love and affection, was as paradisical as possible under the circumstances. Given the location of her father's quarter section of land (even today it remains uncluttered by civilization, rolling and varied under that astonishing, mesmerising Saskatchewan sky); given what she later told me was her close and happy relationship with her older brothers and sisters; and accepting Wordsworth's vision that there "was a time when meadow, grove, and stream . . . did seem apparelled in celestial light," Annie for a time enjoyed life the way only a child can. A sensuous woman herself who understood the immediate world through touch and taste, smell and sight rather than through reason and analysis, she carried those few years forever, however attenuated and brittle they became in her mature life and old age, like an arrangement of dried flowers gathering dust over the years.

Of all the siblings Annie developed the closest relationship with her sister Tenka, four years older than she, of an age to assume the position of authority and play the leader in childhood games, and old enough to become one of Annie's surrogate mothers. Annie was always looking for Tenka, always wanting Tenka to take her hand, to join her at the sloughs where they tried to catch dragonflies or gather bulrushes or pick saskatoon berries by the coulee. The other children were important to her as well, for they were all the children of the dead Rahila and not Stepmother's children. The relationship between Annie and her half brother and sister remained distant and strained. She almost never spoke of them.

Farm children throughout the world do pretty much the same thing, if they are allowed to play at all. Although the tree-thickened coulee runs like a fissure through the land at one end of the farm, my mother remembered best the slough. Sloughs are water-filled depressions, ponds if you will, of varying depths and colours, centres of vibrant insect and plant and small-animal life. Once she saw a white-tailed deer, front feet spread apart as it lowered its head, lapping the water. *Cerb! Cerb!* she remembered shouting in Romanian, startling the animal away. Yellow-headed blackbirds made the slough their nesting place. Of varying sizes, some originally like small lakes on the prairies edged by tall grasses, catkins and dogwood, thickets of wild berries, sloughs have been reduced in number by agriculture and drought, although many can still be seen in the landscape, some dried-out cavities filled with weeds or marshy, semi-stagnant circles indicating what the prairie must have really looked like before the land was ploughed. Nick and John, she said, rolled up their pant legs and waded in, the bottom muck squishing up between their toes. Being the oldest girl, Tenka was required in the household by the overworked Tinca (the two similar-sounding names are variants of one), especially during the latter stages of her two pregnancies in 1915 and 1919 respectively, more than either Mary or Annie. Farm labour also claimed Nick's time and John's. Even a boy of six can do something useful. There was nothing remarkable about this. Annie herself would be expected one day to spend more time at chores than at play.

Disease and death raced across the country and the prairie provinces in 1918 and 1919. The great influenza epidemic scarcely left a household untouched. As medical assistance, if available, was somewhat slow and remote, and certainly limited by the knowledge of the day, thousands of Canadians died, at least five thousand victims in Saskatchewan alone, a remarkably high figure for a small population. Carried across the land on trains by infected soldiers returning from the European war, the Spanish flu met little resistance. It forced the cancellation of public gatherings throughout the province, including church services in Dysart. One of Samson's brothers, Annie's uncle Anton, suffered from tuberculosis, was in fact institutionalized in the Fort Qu'Appelle Sanatorium and died in 1919, although the cause of his death became confused in my mother's mind with the deaths from influenza of so many people. Not a farm in the region escaped. She had no memory of Anton except that he died, but she did remember being doused with alcohol-based home remedies as a precautionary measure. Throughout the region, families suffered terrible losses of their loved ones. Little more than five years old at the beginning of the outbreak, Annie, like most people in the Dysart community, witnessed human suffering on a wide scale under the breathtaking sky stretching over this new land of extraordinary beauty and disease.

CHAPTER 5

There is no going to heaven in a sedan.

So warm outside, so hot in the church. The air outside bright with breezes and birdsong, the atmosphere inside heavy with prayer and chanting. The light of the sun clear against the church windows, the light of candles gold under the chandelier. Standing so long with the worshippers holding babies, so many babies wrapped in shawls and bonneted in white, whimpering and crying and gurgling, so many mothers, heads covered with scarves, chanting and singing, so many fathers with long-sleeved white shirts and vests, their voices also raised in song, voices deep and high, smooth and scratchy, in tune and out, all of them making a joyful noise, and the priest and cantor intoning prayers to God that Annie's scalp began to itch and sweat.

Under the chandelier suspended like a ball of white fire from the wooden ceiling, the light from its prisms emblazoning the eyes of the saints of blessed memory, the eyes of Jesus and His mother, austere and lidless eyes struck by holy fire, stared out from the iconostasis that rose like a wall of polished wood between the worshippers and the holy of holies. Clad in white-and-gold vestments that reached as far down as his muddy boots, brocaded and stitched with shining stones that Annie had been told were jewels pried out of the Empress Theodora's diadem in Byzantium, a magical, mysterious city she could never locate later on the school maps, a crinkled beard that spread over the jewelled cross around his neck like a dark, ragged tapestry, the priest floated around the altar like one of the dead saints come alive, alternately bowed toward the altar and turned toward the congregation, flicking incense, chanting, the cantor in the side chapel returning responses along with the congregation, and passed through the door of the iconostasis, his voice becoming distant, then re-emerged, swaying the fuming censer on its gold chains, casting incense on the holy book on the altar, the word of God on the throne of God.

Annie breathed in the suffocating, sweet odours of God until her six-year-old head lightened and felt as though it would spin off her shoulders and rise on wings like a magpie dizzy from the waves of incense, then rise higher like the words and thoughts of prayer themselves and waft into the fire of the chandelier. The stink of adoration. God smelled so syrupy and burnt at the same time, like the browned edges of strudel left a bit too long in the wood oven, still sweet and good to eat, but a bitter tang at the edges, a memory of the fire that had softened and cooked the apples in cinnamon and sugar before singeing the pastry. Inhaled, the incense swirled about her mind and heart like a kind of music, the sniff of manure and garlic and human sweat mingling with the fragrance of holiness: smell and sound puffed and jangled out of the golden censer by the priest who approached the crowd, a messenger in seething and crisping gold from God Himself.

The singing of the congregation responding to the priest, their voices also rising to mingle with the prisms of the chandelier before flying out the church dome unto the ears of God Himself who heard even the smallest sound, even the rasping hind legs of a grasshopper, a bird flicking among the leaves of a tree, even the last cluck of a decapitated chicken. The songs and responses rose above the thick smell of melting wax, just as the sins of the body and the world melted away under the roof of God, within the penetrating vision of the saints, painted on wood to remind the people that they were not alone in this world of trial and travails. The saints had witnessed so much, had suffered so much and had found inexpressible, ultimate joy. Was her own mama among the saints? Did she fly with the angels? Was her face painted in gold and blue on the holy screen? So the wax melted and all the sinners were saved, their foul malefactions dripping from the temples of their bodies and falling at the feet of the Lord. The darkness of the church thinning into a strange hazy gold as more candles were lit and sins shrank to the size of pea shells thrown into the trough for pigs to gobble. The candles burned as babies cried and were anointed by the holy water scooped out of the marble bowl, and the candles sank and disappeared, their wavering flames bursting for a final moment of great glory on top of small hot puddles of beeswax, as babies were received into the protective arms of the Church.

Once upon a time, Tată (Father) said, when God and the Devil battled over control of the universe, rabbits and owls, hawks and foxes, chickens and lions, all the creatures of the earth had to choose sides. Like the schoolyard during recess when the children chose sides for their games. The humble honeybee chose God. How furious the Devil—he ranted and raged and burned bright red! He whipped the bee as it buzzed in flight, whipped it hard, so accurate was the Devil with the lash, whipped until the golden torso of the bee darkened with black stripes, a permanent memento of choosing good over evil. So the candles burning in the church were made out of beeswax, so the world would never forget that terrible flight and fight of the bee.

And if Annie flew through a hole in the church roof, she could fly right into heaven itself and meet God face to face in his very best parlour, cool and dusted, greet the martyrs whose faces had been painted and carved on the icons, the countless saints of the past whose now shifting and glowing eyes in the candlelight of the *biserică* pierced right through her skull and saw her secret thoughts. She was surrounded by a cloud of witnesses, souls that had perished for love of God and flitted from cloud to cloud, so many that they surely must collide and smack against each other like grasshoppers clicking against the side of the house, except the saints made no noise, their bodies silenced forever, only the eyes of gold and ruby and fire staring above the congregation and all the mothers bearing their children to the font for the christening.

Tenka and Nick and John and Mary, their hands and faces scrubbed, their best clothes on and warned under no circumstances to get dirty again, hid themselves behind the grown-up bodies somewhere in the church, although Tenka had promised to hold Annie's hand, but here she stood without her sister, next to a stepmother whose severe face looked like an icon. Would the woman never smile, even amid all these babies, one of which was her own, the newly born half brother, also to be christened today, his puckered little face smothered under a lacy shawl?

The baby must be accepted into the church or the Devil would claim him, Stepmother had said this morning when Annie had asked why this day of all days was so special. Even Tată had washed from the waist up, put on his white shirt and cleanest trousers and sat outside the kitchen door scraping the dung off the soles of his boots. God protected the children, Stepmother said, her voice sharp as a harrow's tooth. And could no harm come to them once they entered the church? The Devil was everywhere. Even in the church? No, he could not enter the church. So, to be protected and saved, babies had to be sprinkled by and dipped into the holy water in the *biserică*, bathed before the eyes of God who would imbue the child with His love and mercy and protection.

Some babies died last year during the great sickness, as well as young men and women. She remembered Uncle Anton, stricken not by the flu but by another disease she did not understand. Had he not been bathed in holy water? His head so hot that it turned the colour of flame and not all the water in the house could cool it down. Annie did not understand the blatant contradiction between the evidence of her own eyes and experience, and the words dropping like stones out of her stepmother's mouth. Wrapping the baby in white, Stepmother Tinca brushed past Annie, refusing to answer any more questions. Something was missing, Annie thought, reviewing her stepmother's actions. Water, bathing, even a white cotton towel: but where was the soap? Stepmother had forgotten the soap. When Annie took a bath in the metal tub, after her mother and sisters and brothers, she rubbed herself with a bar of homemade soap, corrosive to the skin, the very devil on dirt. Surely, the priest would require a bar of soap and where would he find such a thing in the church, for Annie could not remember seeing a bathtub under the eyes of the saints. Perhaps Uncle Anton had not been washed in holy soap, his body not clean enough to step into God's parlour, but dirty enough for the Devil. From the larder where Stepmother kept all the kitchen supplies, in a small crock pot she found a chipped and cracked bar of lye-based soap and ran out of the house with it, calling after her stepmother and father, holding the bar of soap high like a golden brick:

"*Săpun! Săpun!*"

Annie did not remember what her stepmother said, but, rare occurrence, her father had picked her up and swung her higher than the trees poking up from the bottom of the coulee and carried her on his shoulders to the gate. The entire family waited for a neighbour, whose baby was also being christened that day, to meet them with his wagon, pulled by two horses over the rutted grid road, neither her father nor the neighbouring farmer having enough money yet to buy one of the new clickety-clack automobiles. So high on her father's shoulders, the constant wind of the prairies blowing blue above her head like an endless sheet on the clothesline of heaven. In the old country, Tată had said, landowners and their agents often rode in covered chairs, the sedans, birch poles slipped underneath, carried by two, sometimes by four, men through the village squares and city streets, the backs of the peasants bent and broken under the burden of the boyar's wealth.

In a wagon, their own bodies shaken and jolted as the wooden-spoked wheels trundled over the ridges of the road leading to the main, somewhat smoother, thoroughfare to Dysart, they could sit as they pleased on the benches and hang on to the sides on the way to church, singing songs, knowing, Tată said, that the voice of the people was the voice of God. For all the pasha's riding in a sedan, the poor reached heaven faster than the rich. God's whispers could be heard in the suffering of the miserable. Annie found that concept impossible to grasp. Even the simpering, hot, last breaths slipping out of a baby's mouth like rabbit's paws scampering over snow before she died. That, too, was God's voice?

So powdery fresh and beautiful all the Romanian babies, soft and puffy like pastry in their knitted and crocheted white bonnets and shawls, stitchery like sparrow's feet sewn on the collars of their baby clothes, so delicate the touch and sheen of their unmarked skin, not yet dark and rough or wrinkled, warts sprouting like miniature mushroom caps on the nose, on the brow, on the chin of some of the men and women. Stepmother said Annie wasn't beautiful, for one-half of Annie's mouth seemed to have wrenched itself into a permanent scowl even when she felt happy. Her teeth grew uneven and crowded, pushed against and overlapped each other. Not always a cooperative child, she was too prone to dreaming and keeping her thoughts to herself as if she were thinking things that did not bear thinking about; Stepmother said she didn't like the look in Annie's eyes, something like a crow peering through the leaves for a shiny object to steal like an earring or a wedding band.

Annie had no desire to steal anything, but the word "crow" would stay with her all her life like a knife embedded in stone. *Cioară*: the dark, thieving bird, the black bird, the bird of night, the bird associated with cunning and dishonesty, the ill-omened bird of death. Stepmother had used the term as a joke, but later Annie's aunt and other members of the community would pick it up like a horse brass in the ditch and use it against Annie over and over and over until, in their eyes, she became defined by something they distrusted and wished to reject.

Today, though, was not a day to think about nasty birds, but a day to celebrate, and even Annie's stepmother, not famous for joviality, had spent days preparing the food, as so many women of the community had. Romanians love feasting and communal dinners. In a society where diet and nutrition do not mean abstemious self-denial and fear of fat, the Romanians, when the ingredients are readily available, rejoice in the exquisite pleasures of eating, even at the risk of gaining weight on their bones and elevating the cholesterol in their blood. "Family" and "feasting" are virtually interchangeable terms in the Romanian psyche. Food involves more than mere nutrition or sustenance. Listening to the men and women sing one *doină* after another,

Annie smeared her mouth with *dulceaţă*, the taste of which is determined by the fruit available for its preparation. Essentially a jam, it's made of whole fruit and often eaten with a glass of water. No gathering is complete without heaps and mounds of *mămăligă, tocană de peşte, sarmale, salată de vinete, cozonac, kifull, uscatele, ciroshti, răcituri, porc cu varză* and other foods, on platters and pans, in bowls and crock pots. Feasts of one kind or another accompany every stage of the Romanian child's life, from christening celebrations at birth to the funeral dinner after burial. In the early years of Romanians in Canada, the old culinary customs flourished, not yet modified by or eventually lost in the larger non-Romanian world.

Annie absorbed the recipes and lessons of food just as she absorbed the dislocations and shocks of her childhood. As she related these stories about her childhood, my mother was often seasoning a stew, kneading dough or making cabbage rolls. Her hands always busy, she evinced astonishing knowledge of food and its preparation. She knew how to cook Romanian the way some concert pianists know how to play a concerto in their fingertips. Without consulting a score, they feel the music pulse through the flesh and blood of their hands. Without consulting a recipe book, Annie remembered how to cook one dish after another the way she remembered to breathe. There was no point asking her for the recipe of anything. She knew, but she could not describe how she knew. Giving some obvious ingredients, like flour and sugar and water, she always left out the magical details, the reason why a thing became what it was, the details lost in the magical phrase "a little bit of this and pinch of that." In "this" and "that" lay the miracle of taste, texture and smell.

Not every dish was fit for or even offered to a king. As in many cultures, the food eaten by the peasantry was not eaten by the aristocracy. No food eaten by Romanians in Canada symbolized class differences and social rank or went to the heart of the peasant stomach more than the simplest dish of all, *mămăligă*. Annie learned to prepare it as a child—no great mystery to its preparation in any case—and cooked it for most of her life, no matter how far from her father's sod house she travelled. Other foods come a close second and third in cultural significance—beets, for example, and of course cabbages. But despite the origins of corn, *mămăligă*, in English so unpoetically referred to as cornmeal mush (hardly the sound or consistency or image to tempt the superior palate), is quintessentially Romanian, an argument for cultural cross-fertilization if there ever was one.

One of the curious ironies of world history is the role of corn in the Romanian peasant's diet. A grass grown in the Americas possessing great significance for any number of Aboriginal peoples, corn was transplanted to Europe by Columbus and succeeding Spaniards and Portuguese and shipped along the Mediterranean trade routes. The Turks, who controlled the sea in the fifteenth and sixteenth centuries, intercepted and raided the galleons. Keeping the gold and silver and other precious cargo but indifferent to unfamiliar kernels, they distributed the corn to their subject peoples, like the Romanians. Its symbolic and nutritional properties were ill understood for a long time, and perhaps because it was an important food for the American Native peoples, corn soon became fodder for Eastern European livestock.

A connection was inevitably made. Feed a cow, feed a peasant; after all, peasants were often seen as little better than beasts of burden themselves. This was a notion that remained current well into the twentieth century. Olivia Manning's heroine, fashioned by British arrogance and paternalism, expresses disgust with both Romanian peasants and *mămăligă* in the writer's

Balkan Trilogy novels. Although the symbolic and dietary properties of corn resonate among many cultures, a Romanian mother
in turn-of-the-century Dysart, Saskatchewan, wasn't thinking of
the symbolic connotations so much as the necessity of feeding
her young when she stirred two or more cups of water for every
cup of cornmeal in her pot.

For a porridge-like consistency, stirring and temperature are of
paramount importance. The cornmeal should be poured slowly
from the box (by the handful, to use my mother's method, for she
rarely cooked what she hadn't first touched—modern food pack-
aging a nightmare), each addition stirred and well mixed before
the next, over a heat that allows for dissolution of the grain and
thickening of the mixture without burning. Then, once the
desired consistency has been reached and salt to taste has been
added, the pot is removed from the heat and allowed to stand.

Another method calls for pouring the cornmeal directly into
the boiling water in the centre of the pot, allowing the mixture to
simmer for fifteen minutes without stirring, then submitting the
mixture to a fury of stirring on higher heat for five minutes.
Served hot with cream of chicken or other saucy meat dishes,
mămăligă looks like a mound or square of gelatinous gold on the
plate as if King Midas had brushed his fingertips over the food.
Served cold, if the mixture was not stirred to produce a porridge,
it becomes a kind of unsweetened cornmeal cake, sometimes
sprinkled with sugar or milk. To slice, use a taut thread, not a
knife. Dollops of sour cream or rivulets of maple syrup, not necessarily available and/or affordable then, enlivens the flavour
now. Cheap and easy to prepare, capable of feeding many in a
household crowded with children and loaded with carbohy-
drates for energy, *mămăligă*, despised by the aristocracy, saved
the peasantry from starvation.

Under tea towels sewn from flour sacks, mounds of cold *mămăligă* sat in white enamel bowls on the trestle tables placed in the yard under the young poplar trees. Besides the cornmeal, women who had stayed away from the christening service to organize the feast and set the plates carried out brown bowls, heavy and steaming with *sarmale*, without which no Romanian feast of the people would be complete. *Mămăligă* was all very well—they ate it every other day or more often—but *sarmale*, now that was a relative rarity, so dependent on solid cabbages and the availability of ground beef and pork and tomatoes. With these ingredients, it's obviously a dish more naturally concocted in the late summer and early fall than in the spring when cabbages, if any remain, have been stored too long to create satisfactory cabbage rolls. Every ethnic community of Southeastern Europe boasts a cabbage roll, and one of the minor controversies of cultural history is which people produce the best cabbage roll. My mother, when comparing as she often did, raised an eyebrow over the culinary efforts of Hungarians and Serbians, her own ethnocentricity showing its colours.

A labour-intensive food, *sarmale* is successful only if the proper proportions of beef and pork, mixed with cooked rice, are observed. If the secrets of spice are understood and their relation to tomato broth in which the rolls must cook and simmer for however long it takes, a truly remarkable cabbage roll is created. *Sarmale* is not merely meat, sometimes mixed with rice, and rolled up in a leaf. It's also aroma, spices, juices, flavour, human effort and love. No Romanian mother undertakes the time-consuming task of cooking cabbage rolls, matched only perhaps by the creation of the strudel *plăcintă* in terms of labour, if her heart is not overflowing with love for her family. Then, of course, the art of folding previously steamed, partially cooked cabbage leaves around a roll of meat, the ends tucked in so as not to come undone, is acquired only with practice and perseverance. But what spice, what measurements: it all comes down to "a little bit of this and a pinch of that." *Sarmale* can be eaten with sour cream as well, or allowed to absorb the redolent, spicy tomato sauce in which it has been simmering for hours.

In addition, there were jellied pork hocks or *răcituri*, several pigs having been strung up and scraped the week before, their bellies slit open to drain the blood and remove the innards. Parts of the butchered bodies had been smoked for the winter, but the pigs' feet were now served in metal pans. Boiled in several quarts of salted water for hours until the meat has separated from the bones, seasoned with paprika and garlic, *răcituri* is eventually eaten in its own congealed, fat-soaked broth, set like a jelly in the cold cellar or in the refrigerator. As unappetizing in appearance as in description and chock full of cholesterol, it's not a Romanian dish calculated to appeal to the finer sensibilities of the modern age.

On the wagon ride home, her head light from the smell of wax and incense of the church, the eyes of the saints visible in the clouds that scudded and swirled like skaters in veils across the prairie sky, Annie was given the responsibility of holding a newly christened baby for some of the time. Stepmother held another and chatted with two or three of the women in the Romanian way, nasal voices, all together, using their hands for exclamation points and occasionally crossing themselves as if to ward off the evil eye. Annie's stomach turned to thoughts of food and Tată's promise to play the *tilinca* and to let her join in the dancing of the *horă*. Tenka promised she would not lose sight of her sister Annie this time and would help to look after Mary. Nick would tumble about the coulee and slough after the feast with the other boys, she knew, preferring not to dance, and John, forever fidgeting and restless, would wander off alone, much to Tată's annoyance at times. But even the boys would stay in the yard long enough to eat the food, especially the *plăcintă*, the *cozonac*, the sugary *uscatele* shaped like the ears of rabbits and the nut and date *kifulls*, all of which Annie knew would be served.

Romanian desserts are gravitational in impact. Rich as the earth. They pull one down to the ground, astonished by their savoury richness and texture and determined to keep one's mouth firmly fixed on the matter in hand. There is no better way to consume oily *plăcintă* than eating it by hand, knives and forks and spoons being an aristocratic affectation around these buns and strudels. Unlike French or Austrian cream puffery, so delightful to the palate, Romanian desserts fill the stomach and satisfy the soul's desire for substance and sweetness at the same time. Eat a *madelaine* or *napoléon* and one tastes heaven, to be sure, but so evanescent is the experience that it leads to gustatory oblivion. The stomach soon forgets what it has digested.

Annie developed an instinct for Romanian pastry, first awakened in her stepmother's kitchen and later developed in her aunt's between blows to the head. As with any form of art, instinct is at least as important as practical skill. A little bit of this and a pinch of that: unrecorded, intrinsic, undefinable, occasionally whimsical and always subjective. And if learning to cook well in her aunt's kitchen helped to delay, if not prevent, savagery that could explode without warning, without cause, then added calories (no Romanian woman cooked without tasting a lot along the way) also added armour.

The travelling photographer, jacket off, sleeves rolled up to his elbows, waited by the gate, smoking a brown cigarette. Earning a living by riding the grid roads of the province, knocking on farmhouse doors and amazing the still-inexperienced and recently arrived immigrant with the not-so-new technology of photography, he took baby and family portraits and photographic records of memorable occasions. He had driven from Fort Qu'Appelle in the morning, arriving an hour early; his camera, draped in black, rested on its tripod and leaned against his side. The women looked askance. Stepmother Tinca blushed. Romanian men rarely, if at all, rolled up their sleeves outside as it was considered a form of undress, inappropriate in public, verging on the indecent. In the picture taken by this photographer, not a single man has rolled up his sleeves. Most are wearing white shirts, in honour of the occasion. Women hide their bodies behind voluminous skirts and blouses and kerchiefs.

His car, also black, and roofless, attracted Annie's attention immediately, for she saw and heard the chugging and stinky backfiring machines only on the dusty main road of the village of Dysart or parked alongside the church on Sunday. Developing a love for the Sunday drive in later life, she herself would never learn to operate a car, but so few Romanian women did at the time. Wanting to go, she always stayed. Dependency on a man for locomotion stalled her travelling plans. My mother said she couldn't remember any woman she knew behind the wheel of a motorized vehicle except a tractor.

Perhaps the last glorious time of her childhood, that summer day of 1919, the last memory that decades later still gave pleasure, was the dance, the music, both associated with her father. Having been sorted out and arranged, some standing, some sitting, some lying on the ground, the several Romanian families, not one of the adults born on Canadian soil, are snapped and sealed for posterity in a fading photograph. The photographer clearly had to wait longer than he would have wished, because the picture was not taken before some of the men had quenched their thirst and offered a toast to the newly christened babies and their families.

Annie enjoyed a drink or two in later life, never enough to intoxicate, just enough to loosen restraint like an unlaced corset so she could laugh freely. By then she had reverted to standard rye and ginger ale, or gin and lime, favourites when she could get them, which wasn't all that often, but she remembered both *țuică* and *bragă*, Romanian beverages of the stupefying kind if drunk to excess. When Tată drank, he overcame his natural shyness and tendency toward silence in crowds and sang or played the pipe that he had carried overseas. Like his farm and all of his possessions, the instrument also disappeared from Annie's life. She had nothing tangible to remember her parents by, particularly her father, except the two photographs. Having lost everything as a child, she developed an enormous sense of acquisitiveness as an adult.

Plums were not immediately available to Romanian immigrants in the new land, so the plum brandy or *țuică*, if made at all, would have been rare and rationed. *Bragă*, however, was a different matter. Surrounded by fields of grain, Romanians, willing to replace one beverage with another but not to sacrifice the joy of libation, brewed the drink freely. Made from honey and fermented rye, *bragă* warms the soul and loosens the limbs and tongue, an ideal combination for dancing and jocularity. Stories survive to this day of the availability of homemade stills, technically illegal, in some Romanian households of the region during the twenties. Illegal, perhaps, but one cannot view the matter as criminal.

Many ethnic folk dances have since become self-conscious, precious or embarrassing, or all three. Various cultural groups don their national or regional costumes and dance at one special occasion or another, the quaintness of the exercise proportional to its cultural irrelevance. I'm not referring to show dances whereby the Ukrainian or Irish or Cossack dancers astound a paying audience in a theatre; after all, show business in national costume is not the village dance. One has to make a special effort to dance like one's ancestors, the unnaturalness of the endeavour emphasized by the unfamiliarity of the steps. The ethnic dance loses its cultural significance when performed outside its place of origin. No longer spontaneous or expressive, the ethnic dance suffers from deracination. Uprooted, it wilts and does not recover from transplant shock.

The Romanian *horă* used to be as familiar to Romanians in Canada as *mămăligă*, and certainly my mother remembered dancing the *horă* as a young child before her father died and later in her youth. The dance became associated with the memory of her father and with his smell. Decades after his death, she remembered the odd, heady mixture of tobacco and *bragă*, her father's breath smelling of honey and alcohol. He had held her hand a lot that day, had carried her in the dance on his shoulders; the rarity of the event fixed it forever in her mind. So shaken and jolted by the *horă*, she had been half-fearful and half-exhilarated, her voice drifting into a whisper of nostalgia. Given her position on her father's shoulders during the dance, Annie saw the sky itself tip in a frenzy, the clouds assuming the shape of dancers, the sun a blinding tambourine jangling in gold. "I was close to heaven then," Annie said. What child wouldn't have been? Food, music, physical exhilaration, the unstinting love of a father, a beloved sister who had promised always to look after her, two brothers who played with her in the sloughs and coulees, and Mary who shared her love of stories. Life was complete; she was happier than a Turkish pasha in a sedan. And the dance just whirled her spirits into the sky.

Performed in a linked circle, the *horă* symbolizes community and harmony, inviting those within the village, as it were, and excluding those without. The *horă mare*, the great *horă* (and there are others), is danced on grand occasions like weddings or, as in this particular instance, a christening feast and party. It can be a dance of men or a dance of women or both: a dance of young unmarried women and a dance of young men in need of a wife. Like a circle, it is a dance of beginnings and endings so intricately connected that the former merges into the latter. As continuity is the operating principle of life, so is the *horă*. Still very close to their Romanian roots, the Corches family and their friends and neighbours would have instinctively struck the first chords of the *horă* on their various instruments under the Saskatchewan sky and linked their arms. The tempo of the *horă* can vary from slow and measured to lung-bursting speed. One celebrates until one collapses. Physically demanding, a Romanian dance of celebration is not for the faint-hearted or weak of legs.

Annie's sister Tenka also joined in the dance, although her brothers disappeared and she didn't remember Mary on the occasion at all. For a brief time, my mother danced on her father's shoulders, laughing at Tenka, who sometimes threw bits of *mămăligă* at her sister until their stepmother intervened, appropriately, of course. But in later life Annie shrugged as if to say, what could you expect from a woman who never laughed? Her memories broken and shaped by the events and disappointments of later life, Annie often sighed when she told a story, as if lifting a load off her shoulders and setting it down to rest before resuming the daily burden of her life. So, it was possible to be carried aloft in happiness and love, if for only as long as it takes the earth to turn away from the sun.

CHAPTER 6

Yesterday will not be called again.

In the late summer of the next year, Samson complained of stomach pains, which occurred with greater frequency in September, some days more severe than others. Never one to complain about his ailments and lacking both time and money to consult the doctor in Cupar, he said the pain was little more than indigestion caused by spicy sausages, which he loved and ate every day, although his appetite had waned. What he did eat, he occasionally vomited in the yard. Annie remembered seeing him once doubled over a hand plough, holding his stomach and retching in the field. Frightened by his sickness and assuming that silence obliterated fears, she told no one. She thought he was suffering from the influenza that had stricken and carried off so many people two or three years ago. Just the other day, she heard him tell Tinca not to fuss over him; he was sorry he had even mentioned the pains. One night, wakened by agony in his abdomen, Samson got out of bed and went to the icebox for the pitcher of milk, thinking a cup would assuage the pain.

Samson had poured the milk directly this morning from the pail through cheesecloth to strain out the strands of grass and grain that had spurted out of the cow's teats with the streams of yellowy white liquid. She had watched, asking him to squirt milk into the mouth of the two or three farm cats who appeared and disappeared at will. Like many a peasant, she disliked and distrusted cats but would not see them go hungry. On the farm they helped to control the rodent population. Annie, hearing her father's muttering and stirring in the next room, got up herself, careful not to disturb Tenka and Mary who shared her bed.

It was cold in the house, the fire in the cookstove having died and the chill of November deepening each night. Covered with hard frost, the ground outside would crunch beneath her feet in the morning. She shivered in the nightgown stitched by her stepmother out of flour sacks and embroidered with flowers and birds on the sleeves. She saw her father's arm shake violently, and he dropped the pitcher. It cracked apart and milk spilled on the floor. Reaching down to wipe it up with a floursack towel, Samson lost his balance and slipped. As he fell forward, the side of his head smacked against a corner of the wood table, making a sound like the thud of a wheat sack heaved onto the back of the wagon.

"Tată?"

He did not respond, a hand grabbing hold of the table for support, wiped clean that very evening after Tinca had floured it to knead the bread dough. Annie saw the blood like narrow laces streaming down his cheek, his eyes black in the moonlit kitchen, his face yellowy white like the spilled milk. He remained half kneeling on the floor, his arm resting on the table, the blood dropping like rose petals into the pool of milk, the other arm pressed against the pain in his stomach. He didn't make a sound, Annie recalled; in agony her father remained silent.

"Tată?"

Then she was yanked backward and told to go back to bed by her stepmother, who appeared in a white gown, the collar and cuffs embroidered with red and cobalt blue threads, patterns of remarkably feathered birds perched on plum trees growing all the way from the hem to the bodice. For years Annie remembered Tinca's nightgown. Looking back, she saw Tinca hovering over Samson, wiping his face with the milk-soaked towel and helping him to sit up. Her father leaned over the table, holding the cloth to his temple, which was still bleeding, rocking his body silently in the moonlight.

The next day he disappeared into the fields before she saw him. As she now attended school, Annie was preoccupied for most of the day until late afternoon when she returned home and greeted her father standing in front of the black wood-burning kitchen stove, dressed in his best white shirt and vest, the side of his head covered with blood-stained towelling. They were going to the doctor's in Cupar, Tenka said. First they needed to go to Dysart to ask someone to drive them in a car, one of the few in the community, to the doctor's office. The injury to the head was too severe for their stepmother to heal. So it must have been very bad indeed because one didn't travel to the doctor for minor ailments or insignificant injuries. They were tended to by the woman of the household or ignored altogether, letting nature take its alleviating course.

Silenced by the signs of pain on her father's face, by the clenched taciturnity of his demeanour, Annie said nothing as a neighbour drove his wagon into the farmyard. She ran to the nearest slough in the middle of a field and cried by the browning and frostbitten cattails. The days were cold now, getting colder every day, some mornings so sunny that she was fooled into thinking summer had returned. Stepping outside in the icy winds and sunlight frozen on the beam, she was reminded that winter arrived fast and often furiously in Saskatchewan. Frost spread over the land in the morning like a thin dusting of powdery sugar on her favourite buns. Tenka was old enough to look after the house and make breakfast for the children the next morning, Stepmother said, because it was more than likely she and their father would not return before noon the next day. *Mămăligă* was sitting in a white enamel bowl under a towel in the cupboard. They could eat that and the rest of the bean soup for supper. Cold cheese *plăcintă* for dessert, but they were not to eat it all—leave some for their father tomorrow.

Tinca crossed herself several times as she spoke, her voice thin like frost and cool as the sunlight. She had already shaped the bread dough into four loaves but would not be home to put it in the wood oven. Could Tenka be trusted with the stove's fire? Why give the Devil an opportunity? No, punch it down, wrap it tightly and let it sit in the coolest part of the pantry to slow down another rising. Then punch it down again and again. It could wait until she returned home tomorrow with their father, who would be happy and well again. The boys, including her children by her first marriage, could look after the farm animals and manage most of the chores until their parents returned. Look after the children, Tenka, and baby Eva—don't forget to feed her—and see to it that little George, a bit of a five-year-old nuisance, stayed out of trouble. Eva had been born just a year before, her father's second child by Tinca. George Annie ignored and forgot. Unlike *mămăligă*, love wasn't really something that could be sliced with a taut thread and distributed in nutritious hunks. She had only so much, just enough for her own brothers and sisters. But Eva came along after her brother anyway, and Annie didn't understand how Tată could really love the strange baby.

Her father returned home early enough the next morning, even before the cold sun rose above the wheat fields. Tinca hung up her coat, put on her full-sized apron that covered the entire front of her dress, a deep pocket stretching the width of the skirt and out of which Tinca pulled threads, needles, packets of seeds and spices, strands of lace and even an egg! She prepared breakfast for the children and got them ready for school. His head was properly bandaged, his eyes blacker than a crow's in the ashen yellow of his face. Don't bother your father, Tinca said, but Tată loved his darling Annie. Knowing he did not feel very well, she hadn't expected him to pick her up and dance the *horă* in the kitchen. When she grabbed his legs and hugged, he almost toppled over as the pain in his stomach shot right up to his mouth and exploded in obscenities. Never before had Tată sworn at her.

Tinca pulled her away, and Samson disappeared into the room on the other side of the kitchen where he and Tinca slept. The house was still cold, and Annie shivered over the bowl of *colivă*, the porridge Tinca made for breakfast. She had always hated *colivă* and refused to eat. She went to school hungry, but who could think of food when Tată had pushed her away and sworn? All the way to school, she asked her sister Tenka if Tată loved her anymore, and Tenka just called her silly and told her not to dawdle. They would be late; it was too cold and too early to talk about love. What a child she was, what a crybaby. Besides, Tată just had a headache. Didn't she see the bandage on his head? It would go away soon enough. But did people travel all the way to Cupar and pay a doctor just for a headache?

For years my mother believed that Samson died from the blow to the head, that striking the table had caused a kind of cranial rupture that, although superficially stopped by the bandage, continued to bleed inside his skull. She said that he "died from blood on the brain." Injuries to the head became a strange leitmotif in my mother's memories, perhaps originating in her father's accident in the kitchen. She would also believe that her brother John died from head injuries sustained in a fall from a train. There she confused the facts that blurred over time. In her stories John became almost a mythical figure, the boy who disappeared from time to time on the rails, returning from places unknown, only to depart faster than he devoured a plateful of *mămăligă*, the train an irresistible temptation and force to which he succumbed.

That she was later struck over the head many times by her aunt, and also suffered a head injury in an incident with a horse in the field, deepened her fantastic obsession with "blood on the brain." One of the oddest ironies in this matter was the death of her older brother, Nick, whom she almost never mentioned. He died from a brain tumour at the age of forty-eight, many years after she had last seen him.

Annie never knew the real cause of her father's death. Not that it mattered, for his death struck at the very core of her being and dislocated her sense of self and her place in the world forever. Seven and half years old, she felt his passing in the marrow of her bones as though she herself had died and been buried when they lowered his coffin into the ground.

Samson, in fact, died of stomach cancer on November 26, 1920. With her family and most of the Romanian community, Annie attended the funeral service in the *biserică* and forever after would retain an image of candles flickering under the church windows in the side chapel as the women sang over the funeral bread. The Orthodox church was ablaze with divine light symbolized by the burning candles, the stifling odours of melting wax and flickering smoke mingling with incense and the sweet smell of the bread, which the women would later divide and distribute among the mourners at the great funeral feast after the burial. Her stepmother, surrounded by relatives and friends, her black beaded dress reaching to her black shoes, which she had polished over and over again by the side of the kitchen table until her arms wearied and she let them drop by her side and wept, did not cry in the church.

But in the priest's litany for the dead (*ectenia morţilor*), he said that Tată was not dead but sleeping, and everyone was praying for the soul of the servant of God Samson, who had fallen asleep, *pentru odihna sufletelor adormiților robilor lui Dumnezeu* Samson. Wake up, Tată, wake up. Lord have mercy; *Doamne miluieş te*, Lord have mercy. The simple coffin of wooden planks, hammered together in Fort Qu'Appelle, lay beneath the relentless stare of the cloud of witnesses, the iconic faces of saints, of Jesus Himself, staring over the congregation from the wooden iconostasis as the priest intoned the service, the cantor responding and leading the tearful congregation in dirge. Samson had been popular; the church was crowded.

Tenka, Nick, John and Mary all cried. They, too, had lost their father, although Annie's tears froze like the furrows of the fields in winter. She had wanted to cry, but the tears would no longer fall. She stared at the Mother of God in the iconostasis, Mary's head slightly tilted and bent down to the right, covered in a blue cowl, surrounded by gold. Was she bending her head from grief over the death of Samson? Was she remembering the death of her own son? Annie knew the story, told so often over the years, how the Mother of Jesus had cried at the foot of the cross and later wiped His devastated body in preparation for entombment in the cave. How He had fallen asleep for three days and, joyous to behold, woke up in a blaze of light, light brighter than the candles, all the candles in the church now lit as if struck by the sun, the light they shed a pale reflection of God's infinite light, and the eyes of the saints on the iconostasis looking teary like pebbles under water. Try as she might, Annie could not cry, her heart so heavy that she wondered why it did not fall to the bottom of her stomach.

Members of the congregation shifted forward; some people were walking toward the coffin, partially open to reveal the top half of Samson's body, his head now covered with a black cloth so the wound was no longer visible, his fingers intertwined with a brassy Byzantine cross resting on his chest over his favourite white shirt. With the help of neighbouring Romanian women, Tinca had washed all their clothes in preparation for the funeral, had scoured the white shirt two times with lye-based soaps and starched it until it could practically stand up by itself on the kitchen table. Between the washing, between the sitting down and crying in her apron, the house steamed hot and moist, the air thick with spices and fragrances from all the cooking the women did in preparation for the great funeral feast after the burial. Not only here, but in other houses as well, for a death in a Romanian family is a death in the community and the funeral involved everyone, relative and friend and acquaintance alike. So many people had to be fed. In great grief lay great hunger. Samson should not be shamed in his death. There would also be a rejoicing and celebration among the angels in heaven, happy to receive the blessed Samson. If the Lord Himself would spread a feast for him, why should we on earth grieve forever when the departed has found bliss and plenty above? God gave us food to help us endure the sorrow of living. Annie saw the women roll the meat for the *sarmale*. The cabbages had grown huge and sweet this year. And they spread the dough like a second skin over the table for the cheese and apple *plăcintă*.

Tată's white shirt gleamed, almost reflected in the arms of the cross, his fingers, slightly hairy, unmoving even though Annie hoped they would caress the head of a mourner who had bent down to kiss her father's cheek. One could also kiss the big Bible, encrusted with precious gems, although later she learned the stones were glass and marbles. She was not afraid, like her brothers and sisters, to approach the coffin—not a coffin, for he was sleeping, and sometimes, if he was resting alone in bed, he let the children jump on the mattress to wake him up. He wouldn't want to see her cry. She had cried by the sloughs, had cried in the coulee under the aspen trees, until her eyes hurt and her head grew tense and heavy from sorrow. In the church, under her stepmother's stern and teary face, she did not want to cry anymore, within the fearsome gaze of the saints she did not want to cry anymore, did not want that cloud of witnesses seeing her sorrow.

Some things remained so deeply secret that they sank to the bottom of the earth and would never be dredged up again. Although she could never understand what she was feeling as a child, Annie remembered, even at the age of seven and a half, that she had felt more dead than alive at the time of her father's funeral, beyond fear, beyond grief, even though she would come to regard this time as a form of paralysis. Looking over the rim of the coffin, slightly raised from the floor, she was not afraid to kiss her father goodbye, as was the Orthodox custom. People did so, bending over, crossing themselves. The priest held the great Bible, which looked like a book of gold and jewels dropped from heaven, and far above the congregation glistened the candlelit chandelier, suspended from the middle of the church roof. So much light, so many miniature fires burning at the tip of yellow and white beeswax candles. Honey was indeed sweet, but the bee stung.

Crosses decorated parts of the church wall, and she remembered that the Devil could always lurk behind the cross, even though, strictly speaking, he could not step over the threshold of the church. She approached the coffin, flanked by Uncle Simeon, Samson's last surviving brother, and his old father, Simeon, her grandfather who used to tell stories until he moved away and who now lived in the village of Dysart, much too old to farm anymore, his heart visibly broken. Grandfather Simeon patted her head; she could hear his heavy breathing—not a well man, not a well man at all—and now he needed help to lower the top half of his frail body over the coffin of his dead son.

She stood on tiptoe and extended one arm over her father's

chest to grab hold of the other side of the coffin to steady herself. Uncle touched her shoulders to assist, and she stared into the unearthly blue-white face of her dead father. His eyes closed, no more open to see his darling Ana, see the eyes laughing when she ran to him. How cool the dead face to her lips. Tată's beard was streaked with grey. Unmoving, his body was like that of a sleeping man. Could she waken him, help him out of the bed of his coffin so he could join them at the funeral feast? Let it be a great dinner of rejoicing, for as the stone rolled away from the tomb of Christ, a great blast of light blinded the Marys at the entrance. And the church also glittered and gleamed in polished wood and fiery candlelight. Surely, there was hope yet that Tată, dear Tată, was alive, was not dead, was only sleeping. But why did the priest say, *Intru fericita adormire, veşnică odihnă dă, Doamne*, grant eternal rest, blessed sleep, if Tată really could get up and play the *tilinca* or sing a *doină* or dance the *horă*? And may we never forget Samson, *veşnică pomenire*, the congregation and cantor repeated, memory eternal, memory eternal.

On one side of the church, women held and waved candles over the funeral bread, brown and shining under the light, and sang such a sad song through their noses that Annie wondered how they could sing and cry at the same time. The bread would later be broken for the meal. Uncle and Grandfather led her away from the coffin so others could kiss Samson goodbye. Goodbye, Tată, *adio*, Tată, *Doamne miluieş te*. But still, although her mind had difficulty moving her body like one of the oxen trying to drag a wagonload of wheat over muddy roads, she did not cry, more led and pushed by her uncle and grandfather than walking of her own free will. Above her head the chandelier had become a great blazing circle of light, and the eyes of the saints exploded with fire, and they could see into the very depths of her heart where she had buried her sorrow.

From the church they would walk to the cemetery, only steps away, too short a distance to travel by wagon or car or truck but now too far, impossibly far. With Uncle Simeon holding her hand, Annie walked behind her stepmother, Tinca, who held baby Eva, and in front of Tenka, who told her not to cry, although she wasn't crying at all, not like Tenka and Mary. They walked under the frosty sky now filled by stretches of November cloud, the sky so enormous that birds themselves could never fly to the end of it, her tată used to tease her. With the women dressed in black, shawls over their rounded shoulders, ruffled by the wind like the feathers of crows' wings, their heads bent under dark kerchiefs, and the men in their scratchy brown and black suits, chains of pocket watches dangling from one vest pocket to the other and bouncing on their bellies, the mourners followed the gold-and-white-robed priest to the Orthodox cemetery, some of them carrying icons under that Saskatchewan sky. Ahead of them a great pit had been dug; the earth was hard and crunchy to the touch, but not yet frozen solid enough, not yet frozen deep enough, to resist the spades that dug the hole for Samson's coffin. One day, Annie promised herself, she would fly far away from the graveyard.

Around the burial site the congregation gathered, and the priest spoke more words about sleep and permanent rest and God's servant Samson. In his dazzling vestments whose meaning and origin mythically connected the congregation with the fabulous city of Byzantium on the Marmara Sea, the cross glinting on his chest, the priest stood like a great pillar of light under the grey Saskatchewan sky, intoning words heard as long ago as the time of the Byzantine emperors. So her dear father would never waken at all. Annie tried to tug free from her uncle Simeon's hand, but he would not let her go. She wanted to run, to move, to let the cold wind rush through her clothes so she would feel as cold as Tată's cheek in the coffin, but Uncle Simeon would not release her hand.

Annie did not remember how the service in the cemetery ended, nor did she stay to see the coffin covered with earth. One usually threw a flower in the grave or laid it on top of the coffin, but flowers were scarce this time of the year. Some of the women had woven a wreath of dried flowers and placed it on the lid; others kissed the lid as if it were a person fallen asleep. Uncle Simeon led his niece out of the small graveyard, one of three in the town of Dysart. God insisted there be a separate cemetery for the Orthodox, one for the Catholics and one for the Protestants so as not to confuse Him when it came time to wake everyone up, her father used to laugh, and decide who went to heaven, hell or purgatory, although Tinca warned him not to blaspheme. The Devil had big ears.

Before she left the cemetery, Annie remembered trying to look behind the few memorial stones and crosses in the cemetery, for the Devil crouched in unlikely places. Beware piles of stones, the stories went, for the Devil has a predilection for rubble. Sit on a heap of stones and get pitchforked in the ass. Tinca remained behind, surrounded by women, one of whom had taken Eva in her arms so her stepmother could wipe the tears from her eyes. Somewhere Nick and Johnny, her brothers, had disappeared, probably playing with their stepbrothers among the gravestones, although she didn't think the priest would allow that.

The wind picked up and blew the cold grey right out of the sky like a sheet ripped off the clothesline until her bones shivered and there was no alternative but to wait until everyone was ready to eat. Tată's great feast lay ahead in the church hall. The bread of mourning would become the bread of jubilation. And still, Annie remembered, as if asking for some kind of forgiveness decades later, she did not cry on the day they buried her father.

Part Two

Plăcintă (Strudel)

Dough:

3 cups flour
2 tablespoons shortening
½ teaspoon salt
1 cup warm water
vegetable oil

- *In a bowl, work shortening into flour. Add water a little at a time, using your fingers, until dough is very soft. Continue by pulling and pushing with fingers until dough is smooth and elastic.*
- *Pour a little vegetable oil onto a flat plate or dish and turn dough ball so it is coated. Let dough sit on plate and cover tightly so it doesn't dry out, then cover again with a damp, warm towel.*
- *Let dough rest in a warm place for an hour or two (or up to a half day).*
- *Cover a table with a large cloth rubbed with flour.*
- *Roll dough as thinly as possible. Then, using fingers, start from centre and pull dough gradually outward all the way*

around. Do not let dough dry out. Oil top very lightly, if necessary, to stop it from tearing. Finished dough should be paper thin.

Apple Filling:

8 to 10 apples, peeled and sliced
1 cup sugar with 1½ teaspoons cinnamon added

- Sprinkle dough with vegetable oil, and cover with apples, sugar and cinnamon.
- Starting on one side, roll up dough toward centre. Do the same thing on the opposite side, rolling toward centre. Cut lengths to fit side by side in a large baking pan.
- Bake at 400° F for 35 to 45 minutes until lightly browned.

Serves 12.

CHAPTER 7

He has raised a bird to pick out his own eyes.

On January 1, 1921, Annie's grandfather Simeon died at the age of eighty-three. Not eight herself, she had already suffered the loss of her mother, her father, her paternal grandparents and her father's brother, Uncle Anton, all of whom had been born in Romania. So much death in the immediate family does not go unnoticed even by a child. That she clung to Tenka, her oldest sister, is not surprising especially as Tenka seemed to have developed a maturity beyond her years. Annie's childhood sense of certainty and security was irreparably damaged by the suddenness of her father's death, heightened by the passing of the dear grandfather less than two months later. To compensate, she began dreaming about and cherishing the ideal of a permanent family that she could never approximate in real life, as well as viewing the world through a fatalistic lens. It is obvious to say that nothing good lasts, but Annie took the universal in a personal way. Expect little to avoid being disappointed is a defeatist and corrosive attitude for a child to harbour, but her father's death contributed to Annie's skewed notion of reality. That, and later events, intensified her belief that life consisted of heartbreaking separations, that one's deepest need to love and be loved would always be frustrated and betrayed.

In a household of several children, the five original Corches siblings and Tinca's two children by Samson, not to mention the children by her previous marriage, the burden of care, the demands of the land, the economic imperatives were enough to knock a weaker woman off her feet. However strong, Tinca nonetheless had to look about herself and secure a helpmate. Despite Annie's somewhat cool attitude toward her stepmother, who did not seem to waste either words or love, Tinca had little difficulty in finding a third husband. The woman must have possessed her share of charms or been a very hard worker indeed, a more enviable and desirable trait for the times and place, for she married again, another widower, in July 1921. Given the brevity of the unions, Tinca did not evidently enjoy great good luck in her choice of husbands, something Annie herself, faced with few and narrow options, would experience in adult life. Whether this third marriage was a love match, however one would wish it to have been so, was irrelevant to Tinca's immediate needs. It was simply impossible for her to feed so many children and operate Samson's farm without the help of a husband.

It's interesting to note that not one of Samson's children benefited by his ownership of land, his property passing entirely out of their hands through marriage and remarriage. Division of labour was a solution to Tinca's work, but division of the children even more necessary. For the children not related by blood, the process of removal began. Tinca was not, however, the stereotypical wicked stepmother of fairy tales; she was overwhelmed by her circumstances. Neither wicked nor merely malicious, she was making every effort to look after her offspring. Clearly Tinca did not regard Annie as her responsibility any longer. For a child who yearned to attach herself to a loving parent, even a surrogate parent, the loss of her family home, of the land she loved so much that it remained in her heart to the end of her days, and separation from her brothers and sisters did not enable her to look on the bright side of the wheat field.

Between 1921 and 1924 Annie, although she attended school, lived a kind of borrowed existence. Neither loved nor hated by any parent at all, perhaps despised and resented by adults, hanging on to Tenka's hand, she demanded in a sense that her siblings pay attention to and love her to the point of obsessive fixation. But what was poor Tenka to do? She was herself growing up into young womanhood, and already her thoughts and fancies were turning elsewhere. The brothers, old enough to see the lay of the land in more ways than one, had plans of their own. John was always inattentive to chores and restless, Nick beginning to imagine a life on his own. Childhood, in any case, did not last long among the offspring of immigrant Romanians in early Saskatchewan.

Annie told me that she used to spend more and more time in the coulee at the back of the house, scrabbling her way down to the bottom, scratching her arms, sometimes tearing her clothes, just to feel the insects on her skin and to remember her father. This was a means to get out of the house, not so much to avoid work, which Annie never feared, but to avoid the chill in the kitchen. A child knows when she is not loved, and the feeling came close to being utterly unbearable for my mother. Or she wandered along the dirt grid road looking for saskatoon berries in season, with a view to bringing a pail back home to please Stepmother, a kind of offering or bribe: please don't send me away. Of course, she helped herself to as many of the purplish blue berries as she could stuff into her mouth, forgetting for the moment that Tinca rendered them into jams and pies. Saskatoon-berry pie, its crust honey gold and crimped around the edges with a forefinger or the back of a fork—what texture and magic in the taste. Picking berries always remained a satisfying pleasure for Annie, who preferred in adulthood to go to the nearest "Pick Your Own Strawberries" farm and spend a morning searching for the ripest fruit. The riper the berry, the easier to mash and the sweeter the jam. Her face browned by the sun, a straw hat or kerchief covering her head, she would stand in her cotton flower-printed housedress among the six-quart baskets of berries like a minor domestic deity surveying her fruit.

All the children used to play around the edges of the slough, which froze into a skating rink in winter, but now they played less and less, as if the death of Samson had broken the circle, had irreparably damaged the core of their feelings for one another. What a terrible thing to be orphaned. Some children take it harder than others, some recover and others do not. The commonness of the event, especially at this time, in no way eliminates the psychological devastation.

Odd as it may sound to our ears today, it wasn't unusual then for adults and more fortunate children, Romanian or not, to blame the orphan for her condition. To some degree, Annie internalized the implied criticism and condescending compassion. The way Tinca kept her distance could only mean that she, Annie, perhaps her brothers and sisters as well, bore some responsibility for the death of their father and even their mother. Moreover, the growing realization that she was to be sent away to live with someone else, that she could not be considered a daughter of her father's household any longer, translated into a sense of rejection and, to some degree, self-contempt. Why was she so unlovable that her parents died to escape, that her stepmother had to remove her from the premises? Annie's darkening hair and complexion, typical of many Romanians, combined with a certain sullenness, encouraged Tinca to view the girl as remote and difficult to understand. She was too secretive and sly like a crow, hiding thoughts behind all that staring into space. She also had a tendency to run off to hidden sections of the land and spend a longer time alone than was good or proper. Tinca did not take kindly to crying children, for a sod house was too small to endure a crowd of misery and the bread had to be baked, after all. She had little time to assuage the child's grief over the death of her father.

Annie did not cry in front of Tinca in any case. She reserved the flow of tears for the coulee, or sometimes, very early in the wintery morning, even before Tinca awoke, which must have been very early indeed, she would trudge in the fields as far as she could before her inadequately protected feet got too cold. She liked to feel the cold light of the rising winter sun on the skin of her cheeks, to see the blue shadows of dawn drift like veils over the snow-covered fields. Embarrassed by the memory, she confessed to imagining her father in heaven, parting the clouds or grey shield of the atmosphere, watching his little Annie shiver beneath the enormity of the sky. She raised her arms like wings and attempted to fly, running as fast as she could, often tripping over the furrow and falling in the snow, flapping her arms, the wool scarf wound about her head and face coming loose and trailing down her back like a broken wing. Tată, Tată, Tată!

The cold raced into her lungs, and her words sputtered out in coughs and gasps. Annie ran and tripped and tumbled in the snow, jerking and extending her arms until the muscles, strained and sore from the exertion under the restrictive coat, became leaden and incapable of lifting her off the ground. But her body didn't matter anymore; it was merely a prison out of which her spirit could escape and fly, if only Tată would reach down from the heavens and help. She was the *pasărea maiastra*, the magical, mythical bird of Romania. The *maiastra* sang such a beautiful song, Tată had told her one night, that the dead, wakened by angelic sounds slipping through the soil, rose from their graves and rejoined the living. The idea horrified Annie until Tată had assured her that they weren't ghastly ghouls or vampires. Really a princess in disguise, just like the way Tată had made her feel, the *maiastra* boasted feathers of unsurpassed beauty.

In Samson's eyes, she wasn't a crow, a *cioară*, at all, dark and thieving, sly and deceptive, but *maiastra*, wonderful to behold. The bird's name also meant "thief" but only because she stole from Death and gave back to the living, restoring life to those who had lost it. She could also make the blind see and tell the secrets of the future. The women wove and stitched this wonderful creation, as well as other birds, into their rugs and tapestries as a constant reminder of life and miracle. Her father: not dead, not dead, not buried beneath the frozen ground, but alive, flying, alive and flying like a great beneficent bird, hovering above her head, blocking out the sun in the sky, which was becoming grey with the threat of more snow. Since *maiastra* had restored life to her father in the sky, why, oh why, did he not descend and take up his little Annie once again and press her against his warm heart? Out of breath, panting in the middle of the endless snow, she waited for her father to make a sign in the sky, waited until the sun rose. Over the horizon appeared a pale gauzy light, threaded with gold, and Annie waited until the sun rose and she was late for breakfast, for school, for everything.

In the exhilarating desolation of the Saskatchewan morning, the roll and dips of the churned-up earth, the powdery surface of the snow picked up by the wind and swirling like great drifts of ghostly spirits trying to reach the unattainable sky, Annie repeated a *doină* that her father had sung, the parts she remembered, as the sky lifted and her eyes almost hurt from the glare of sunlight skidding off the snow. A dark little Romanian child imagined an ancient, immortal bird connected with the hills and forests of Transylvania, there on the bleak beauty of the

Saskatchewan winter. She searched the sky for evidence of the fabulous bird of resurrection, trying to connect wishful thinking with fact, her sense of remoteness so strong that it struck colder than the wind slapping light and snow against her uncovered face. And my mother would pause as she repeated this story, twisting the handkerchief, staring into a cold cup of tea, as if that childhood memory was too much to utter. Unfamiliar with Brancusi's stylized brass sculpture of the *maiastra*—in which the bird's head is raised, her beak seemingly open to sing a song of resurrection, her body, wings and feet all seamlessly coherent like an exquisite piece of geometry—Annie nevertheless put emotions into the story that were equal to the feelings and traditions the sculptor shaped into his art. Then Annie showed me her most recent doily, the centrepiece a bird with widespread wings of blue and white lace caged in a delicate circle of fine threads out of which it could not fly.

In an angry moment, for where there is little humour there is often suppressed rage, Tinca spoke harshly to Annie for dawdling, for inattentiveness, for laziness. You were no help to Tată, she charged more than once, an accusation that sank as deep as an icicle breaking off the edge of the roof and disappearing into a bank of snow. It did not, however, melt. My mother remembered the comment all her life. Annie didn't have the impression that her brothers and sisters withered under her stepmother's attitude. That may have been true, or Annie, at this earlier age, began evincing a self-involvement that deepened as she matured and led to constant comparisons between the sufferings of others and her own, as if to confirm no matter how bad someone else's life, she could find something worse in her own. So wrapped up in her own unhappiness, she saw little of how Nick or Tenka, John or Mary, must have felt at the time. They, too, had lost their loving father. Self-regard is not an attractive quality, admittedly, perhaps originating in childhood self-pity, but more than likely in self-recrimination. Like many orphans, the child believed that she must have been detestable and guilty of some unspecified crime. Yet the ravenous need for love that none of her brothers or sisters could truly satisfy became so tangible that it struck like hunger pains in Annie's stomach.

The separation of siblings after the death of their parents, with unwanted children placed in foster homes, was a fairly common occurrence. In their decisions regarding the welfare of these children, adults more often consulted their own convenience rather than the child's feelings and wishes. Annie drew some temporary solace at least from still living on her father's land with her sisters, Tenka and Mary, and her brothers. If Tinca lacked room in her house or love and consideration for her second husband's children, so did everyone else. It was impossible to find a local family to take them all in. Life was hard, rewards few, money limited, children many. Everyone had a row to hoe. One of Samson's sisters, Sophie, now the wife of a prosperous farmer, had married young and given birth to several children by the time her brother died. For a while the boys may have resided with Samson's last surviving brother, Simeon, and his wife, Eudora, who had no children of their own. Annie may have lived in his house for a few weeks as well. Barely nine years old, Mary was sent to a foster home, either in Weyburn or Estevan.

An extraordinary event occurred in Annie's life at this time, one she rarely spoke about, and one that can only be put together small piece by small piece. Certain pieces are forever lost, for none of the transactions were stamped, signed and sealed in any formal registry office or institution. But the children, two of them at any rate, were certainly delivered to, of all places, Helena, Montana. A long black car pulled up the dusty driveway toward the house. Her stepmother stood on the thresh-old, wiping her fingers covered with sticky flour (Stepmother was always kneading dough) and greeted a man whom Annie had never seen before. She and all the other children had been washed under the pump in the kitchen—scoured is a more appropriate term—until her skin burned from the rubbing and turned the colour of beet soup. An exaggeration to be sure, although washed she certainly was, for no Romanian woman would present the dirty face of a child to a visitor.

More than likely it was a Ford coupe, essentially a box on wheels in the style of 1920, rather than the long black car of her imagination. Annie was transposing a limousine of later decades, a funeral car, onto whatever vehicle had driven up to the farmhouse in the late spring or early summer of 1921. The funeral car symbolized how she felt on that most horrible day. Soon to marry again for the third time, Tinca would also leave her second husband's home. Samson's farm would be rented or sold or simply become part of her new husband's domain.

Annie and her brother were driven in the great black coffin of a car, to quote my mother's metaphoric misconception, to live with their grandparents, Rahila's mother and father, in Montana. Annie knew nothing about her mother's parents. Samson had never mentioned them. She had not known they even existed. It wasn't likely that Samson would have corresponded, and there was no telephone in his house, although the first telephone office was installed in Dysart in 1911, the year of her brother John's birth. Given Samson's lack of education, his unceasing preoccupation with establishing a farm once his wife died and the distance between the communities, Samson had neither need nor means to remain in touch with Rahila's parents who, instead of immi-grating to Canada, had taken a different boat and lived a different life in the United States.

Someone in the Romanian community must have been in contact with them, possibly Uncle Simeon, who also had never spoken about his sister-in-law's parents to his niece, or the village priest, who would have been literate and knowledgeable about the comings and goings of many Romanian families in Dysart and elsewhere. They lived, as far as Annie was concerned, at the end of the world, a place she did not wish to go. One box, a crate of sorts similar to the kind of box used for shipping eggs, had been mysteriously packed for her the previous night and was resting under the kitchen table next to Nick's. When she understood the purpose of this strange visitation, Annie ran out of the house, with Tinca screaming after her to come back. Nick, who knew his sister's hiding places on the farm, traipsed after and discovered her crying in the coulee. She tried to break free of his hand and searched through the tangled branches of the aspen trees and bushes, spotted a yellow-headed blackbird and screamed *maiastra, maiastra,* all to no avail. There was no help from the magical bird. Nor did she see her father's face in the scurrying clouds of the sky. The perpetual wind of the prairies rushed through the grass and made it sing.

She could have borne everything, except the loss of Tenka, who would go to live in Regina, a city Annie knew only by name and so far away it might as well have been Byzantium. Tenka embraced and kissed her and told her to be brave, they were all going to a new home, wasn't that wonderful, to people who would care for them. When Annie cried, resisted, she was almost dragged into the car with Nick. Scrabbling up the back seat to look through the rear window, she pressed her fingers against the glass, trying to push it out, and saw the world of the farm through too many tears. No one remained outside. Tenka had already disappeared into the house. Not even her stepmother had stayed outside long enough to wave goodbye. Mary and John, too, had vanished. Sharing the fate of thousands of children around the world, then and now, who have lost their families, Annie felt no less severely. How is it possible to measure and evaluate the emotional wrench?

The yard was empty and the sky went on forever and forever, the clouds thickening and drifting and seeming to travel faster and faster away from her sight. On the roof of the house her father had built, the house that sometimes rained mud in the spring or sagged and sighed under the weight of snow, she saw a great black crow pecking among the thatch, the sun glinting off its wing, getting smaller as the car slowly negotiated the ruts of the road. No, it wasn't the magical bird to bring her back her life, this sudden bird appearing out of nowhere, as if it had dropped out of the sky. The nearest trees rose seemingly out of a chasm, a distance away in the coulee.

It was the black bird of death, the evil bird, the cunning thief. Crows pecked at the eyes of dead cows in the fields. If the crows fed on the flesh of the eyes, could the *maiastra* restore the sight of cows? The crows had lined themselves like black pins on the clothesline in winter where the frozen clothes and sheets hung like petrified ghosts in the severe sun. In the summer she saw smaller birds dipping and darting in the sky in a concerted campaign against the crows. What is my future, *maiastra*, tell me what will happen to me?

She nestled against Nick's side. Her brother put an arm around her shoulder and told her to stop crying. At least Niculai remained with her and she could cling to him in Tenka's absence, and poor Mary and poor John who'd rather slop about the sloughs than go to school. Where, oh where, would they go? What did the future have in store for them? Tell me, oh magic bird, tell me what will happen to me. Will you bring me back from the land of the dead? And the car, finding a secure track on the rutted road, carried her away. Nick remained as silent as her father's body in the coffin, staring at his shoes, his comforting arm still on her shoulder. The driver, the man with the long black coat, spoke a fast English, too fast for her to comprehend fully, and no one remained in the yard to call her back home, just the spot of crow. Annie loathed the sight of crows for the rest of her life. The Romanian name, *cioară*, would be used to define and taunt the dark little girl who had lost everything she loved.

CHAPTER 8

He that takes a devil into his boat
must carry him over the sound.

Annie persuaded herself to believe that she was being adopted by her mother's parents, total strangers to be sure, but blood relatives who had raised her mother in the old country. She believed that her new and mysterious grandparents would be as loving as Samson's father, who had also told her stories about the magical and sometimes frightening forests and hills of Transylvania where bears and wolves tore down beehives or ravaged the sheep. She believed heartache would be transmuted into happiness at the wave of a magic feather dropped in flight by the golden bird of folklore once she got out of the car in Helena, Montana. As a Romanian proverb so aptly puts it, we soon believe what we desire.

How long it took to travel the distance between Dysart and Helena, Annie did not recall. She did remember stopping at various houses along the way, spending at least one night with a Romanian family who boasted about their fat, speckled hens. Nearly a thousand miles, the journey would have tested the endurance of a Ford coupe. She seemed to believe that she had boarded a train at some point. What Annie did clearly remember was her first sight of mountains, and she wondered how it was possible to grow grain in the foothills. The mountains, however, did not impress. Too much a child of the prairies, Annie regarded mountains as obstacles in the way of land and sky. When she lived for a time in British Columbia as an adult, she did not speak about seeing the mountains.

Finally, when the car stopped at their destination, the driver told Annie to stay in her seat as Nick got out. Getting out himself, the driver then helped the sturdy boy unstrap his crate from the back of the car. Only one crate was removed. Before he slipped off the seat, Nick kissed Annie's cheek and told her to be brave, to remember their father. Annie was too exhausted from worry and despair, and too hungry, to understand what she was seeing. The car had driven up a road into another farm, probably closer in size to a ranch than to her father's quarter section. Although the horizon was blocked by high hills and distant mountains, the sky seemed as grand as Saskatchewan's sky.

On a wooden porch, which her own house in Saskatchewan did not boast, stood two people in straw hats, one a man, one a woman, both old. Her new grandparents, she thought, and to some degree the pain in her heart lessened, for going to grandparents did not seem such a frightening prospect, after all. She moved to get off the seat and out of the car, but the door was locked. The driver got back in behind the wheel. Nick was carrying his crate toward the house, where the old people remained motionless. He put down the crate, turned around and waved. As if he was saying goodbye, which she thought very odd indeed. Such a big boy for his age, Nick, fifteen years old. He would take care of his youngest sister.

The car backed away again and Annie, horrified, leaped off the seat and grabbed the driver's head. The car swerved but continued, although she must have been blocking the driver's view. Stop, you're forgetting me, she screamed, pulling at the driver's hair until the car braked and she knocked her chin against the back of the driver's seat. The driver pushed her arms away. His look sour and severe, his voice harsh like a winter's wind, he told her to sit down. She was not staying here. She went numb from shock, slipping back onto the seat, not turning around this time to look out the rear window, the engine of the car, the rumble of its tires on the road, so loud she could not hear her own sobs. If a heart could be said to stop without killing a person, my mother said, her heart stopped that moment, although she continued to breathe. How was it possible to breathe and be dead at the same time? Her heart was beating in the coffin of her body, and she was feeling nothing, nothing at all, like a man succumbing to sleep under a drift of snow.

Not dead, she was certainly alone in a foreign country, although the sky looked the same. Favouring males over females as farm workers, Rahila's parents had selected only one of her children, the oldest, strongest boy, to help them on the farm. Perhaps the geographic distance from their grandchildren and the many years since they had seen their own daughter had also severely weakened family ties and compassion. Nick could be a useful tool on the land, Annie not—an odd decision, for Romanian women worked as hard as their men on the farm, perhaps harder because they also managed the household, prepared the meals and reared the children. In any case, Rahila's parents, perhaps poor and struggling, had little means to support more mouths than they believed capable of contributing to the work on the farm. They could not even begin to imagine the child's misery. If one chose a child as one chose an ox, thinking solely in terms of ploughing and harvesting, this shy eight-year-old girl would have been a poor choice. Despairing in the back seat of the car, Annie, though, had not been entirely deserted. No one had troubled, however, to inform her of their intentions. She looked to the sky for the appearance of *maiastra*, hoping for some indication of her future. The clouds roiled and mounted furiously that day, a major rainstorm approaching.

In the Romanian community of Saskatchewan, at least in the first few decades of the century, everyone not related to the family soon learned of Tinca's remarriage and the dispersal of the Corches children. Few private telephones were available, although there was an operator in Dysart by this time, but news and gossip nonetheless flew over the land like crows on the wing. Nothing so unsettling could have been kept secret, and there was no reason to be secretive anyway. A father's death, a widow's remarriage, children sent to foster homes: interesting events but hardly shameful or the stuff of secrecy. If adults failed to understand one particular child's shattered heart, they nonetheless had experienced troubles and turmoil in their own families, tragedies also, and most survived to continue with their lives. God was great, but the Devil was also clever, and so, with a Romanian shrug of the shoulders or a crossing of the chest to ward off evil, they acknowledged the presence of misfortune and sorrow on the sunniest day in the Saskatchewan sky and planted seeds anyway.

Supposition, especially when it comes to personal reminiscence, is a seductive and pointless game. My mother sometimes slipped into an odd reverie, supposing how different her life would have been if she had stayed in Montana. Well, the only answer is that her life would have been very different indeed, but the supposition was not the life she lived. The reason for the supposing had to do with the actual foster parents who, unlike Rahila's mother and father, opened their doors to Rahila's last child and received Annie with instant love and affection. Their warmth was rather remarkable when one considers the child's unhappy, sullenly reserved, determinedly cool and unresponsive stance. She had been ripped apart (my mother's words) so often in such a brief time that she was afraid of letting anyone touch her again lest her heart crumble under the impact of affection given then suddenly snatched away. Another rupture would have been unbearable, like the Devil gouging out her eyes on the prongs of his fiery fork. My mother always retained a vivid sense of the Devil's inclinations.

Surprising to learn, my mother's foster parents in Montana were Jews. Annie was an Orthodox Christian girl, a child of Romanian peasants who had left their homeland to escape poverty, taxation, exploitation and the occasional slaughter. That they were anti-Semitic has to be acknowledged, given the history of and attitudes toward Jews in Romania, attitudes that did not deservedly drown on the passage over the Atlantic.

Romanian landlords were called boyars, an indication of Russian influence in the early part of the nineteenth century. At one time, deprived of land, Romanians were either shepherds (hence Clifford Sifton's sartorial reference) or peasants legally bound to the estate by feudalistic laws. Propaganda achieved its purpose in a country where frustration and need combined. Smitten with promises of land and opportunity, Simeon had behind him a history of deprivation and oppression to help him decide to immigrate to Canada. He was not unique.

Between 1881 and the First World War only minor changes in the way of adequate land reform occurred. Anger against absentee landlords living in the cities off the avails of peasant labour or in their mansions on the estates was easily inflamed by earnest reformers and demagogues. Moreover, some of the intermediaries or middlemen between boyar and peasant—estate agents, if you will—were in fact Jewish. Ignited by the deep and enduring grievance against the boyars, poisoned with historical anti-Semitism, rage boiled beneath the bent back of the peasant in the fields. Peasants, like some demagogues, can be bloodthirsty. Close to the ground or nose in the air, the former pitches the fork in the eyes, the latter justifies. This is not the place to explore anti-Semitism, but it is the place to acknowledge its presence in the mind of the peasant. Once aroused by demagoguery against the landlords, the peasants turned not only against Jewish estate agents but against Jews generally. During the rampage against large estates and the slaughter of boyars and their families, the peasants butchered Jews wherever they found them simply because they were Jews. It required no great stretch of the peasants' imagination to confuse devil or injustice with Jew. The Christian peasants' grievance against the boyars became so demoniacally entangled with anti-Semitism that the peasant uprising in 1907 in the name of justice and land reform became yet another horrendous pogrom.

For a very brief time, Annie entered a house where her very nature and character as a child were welcomed and cherished. She was not expected to be more than she was, and apparently every effort was made to secure her comfort, to soothe her fears and to mollify her anger.

Supported by Baron Hirsch, the famous Jewish philanthropist and founder of the Jewish Colonization Society, whose mandate it was to help relocate Jews who were victims of the European pogroms, the majority of Romanian Jews, mostly Ashkenazi Orthodox, immigrating to Saskatchewan at the turn of the century, established themselves in the Lipton area, not far from Dysart. There, they formed an agricultural colony with enough members to build a wooden synagogue, later destroyed by fire. The ruins of the synagogue roof now remain like a sad monument to the past on a private farm outside of the town. The Hebrew Cemetery, no longer used for burials, lies ten miles northeast of the village of Lipton, approximately fifteen miles from Dysart. In the very earliest days of the colonies, the Jews received food from the Native people. The exchange of food between immigrant and Native also became an aspect of my mother's own life when she returned to Saskatchewan.

It's disturbing to remember that the Ku Klux Klan reached as far north as Saskatchewan, into the very tiny settlements of Romanian immigrants where, proscribing virtually everyone not themselves, the members promulgated their anti-Catholic, anti-French and most markedly anti-Semitic lunacy. The homes and cemetery of Jews in Lipton, Dysart and neighbouring Cupar were occasionally vandalized. It's even more disturbing to learn that the government of Canada in its Royal Commission on immigration listened to an anti-immigration report submitted by a branch of the Ku Klux Klan that called for a quota system based on the 1901 census when the presence of Romanians was negligible. Such anti-foreign feeling—also present in briefs submitted by the Grand Orange Lodge of Saskatchewan and the United Farmers of Canada, Saskatchewan section, the latter asking for a five-year moratorium on Southern and Eastern European immigrants—influenced *The Report of the Saskatchewan Royal Commission on Immigration and Settlement* in 1930. The immigrants proscribed therein were of course Eastern European. But these objections, a common English xenophobic attitude of the time, did not substantially affect Annie's life.

For its first two or three decades, the town of Dysart in the middle of the breathtaking Saskatchewan prairie, surrounded by newly ploughed wheat fields and Indian reserves, was essentially a Romanian community, although members of other ethnic groups also lived there. The most common language spoken on the very wide, dusty (or muddy) main street among Christians and Jews alike was the language and its dialectic variants of Transylvania, Wallachia, Dobruja, Moldava and Bukovina.

Dysart itself became a kind of communications centre for the various groups of people and communities. So one didn't have to attend the Orthodox church to learn of a neighbour's death or the homelessness of his offspring. The availability of Jewish orphans in Montana was limited. The connections between Romanian Christians and Jews were close, if often deadly for the Jews. Rahila's parents lived in Helena, Montana, but were still indirectly connected with Dysart and therefore indirectly connected with the entire community. It's not surprising that a Jewish couple in Montana would have heard of children in Dysart who needed a home. Such unofficial "adoptions" were fairly common, given the laxity, ineffectiveness or non-existence of institutional channels and procedures in the early days and the ease with which borders were crossed then. Orphaned Canadian children often became another natural resource for Americans, although it was unusual for American Jews to adopt a prairie Christian child.

Very little is now known of the kind couple who tried to give Annie a home. That she resisted their love and care was regrettable but also inevitable. Her roots embedded in the Dysart farm, her memories of her beloved father and Tenka too strong to allow room for the new life into which she had so suddenly been thrust, she passed her time moping and crying to herself under the Montana sky. Her continuing sorrow did not bode well for her new parents. Perhaps they expected too much of Annie too soon, their need for a loving child as great as hers for a loving family. The shock of separation, of the dissolution of her entire family in a matter of months, rendered Annie incapable of speech or appetite. She went sullen, refusing to eat *mămăligă, sarmale, răcituri, kifulls, colivă* or any other dish the good people served in hope of breaking the child's descent into despair and her resistance to their love. Annie did not recall attending

Orthodox services in Montana, nor was she expected to follow Jewish practices and beliefs.

They gave her new shoes, the first pair she remembered ever receiving. And a rag doll sewn and stuffed by her new mother. The eyes were black sequins removed from the bodice of the woman's best dress. What she hadn't forgotten, though, despite her recalcitrance and tears, was the couple's essential decency. Annie missed Tenka so much that she cried herself to sleep repeating her sister's name. She missed her father, her sister Mary and her brothers, too, but wherever she looked, expecting somehow that they would appear because she wished it so hard that her head ached from praying to God to restore her family, Annie saw no one to take their place. How was it possible to replace those whom she loved? Having loved once, she could not bring herself to love again, although the muscles and nerves of her body yearned for the restoration of her family. Offered love by unfamiliar people, she instinctively rebuffed it.

Exactly how many days and weeks she remained in that Montana household is a matter of speculation, but it wasn't more than three months, long enough for the experience to impress itself in Annie's memory, although she never once in my recollection identified them by name. Nor did she convey any sense of how she passed the days, whether she was enrolled in school, which is doubtful, or she worked on the farm. As she matured, a kind of blanket forgetfulness covered that brief sojourn in Montana, burying the memory of people who had tried to reach her heart. They almost passed into oblivion like the near-extinction of the prairie bison.

But some inchoate, unconscious sense of gratitude remained with Annie all her life, some appreciation and even regret lingered, expressed not in words but in a singular moment of quiet beauty. Years later in Windsor, Ontario, she washed down the wall of a small cinder-block synagogue on the corner of the street where we lived next door to a kosher poulterer's. She often exchanged comments about the weather and the quality of chickens with the butcher. Everyone in the neighbourhood was poor. The stone of the synagogue had been defaced with anti-Semitic graffiti in red and yellow chalk. After she removed two loaves of bread from the oven that very early Saturday morning (the aroma intoxicating, most of the household still asleep), I watched her leave the house, pail and wire-bristled brush in hand. Although told to stay inside and set the table for breakfast, I followed to see my mother standing on the weedy strip of land between sidewalk and synagogue, singing a Romanian song quietly to herself and scrubbing the filth off the wall. She neither commented on my appearance nor explained her actions.

There was nothing for it but to send Annie back to Dysart. Arrangements would have to be made to return the child, but to whom? Every family had more children than the parents could feed and house, so it was said, although Romanians are adept at concocting plenty out of little. Annie had been placed in a fine and loving home. The distress and bitter disappointment caused by her refusal to bow to the inevitable—life in Montana—did not endear the child to some people back home. Annie learned about this resentment because she was constantly reminded of how ungrateful and difficult she had been, what a burden she was to those who were now forced to look after her, the Devil's child herself. As for the Jewish couple, however, who had tried their best, Annie's evident misery broke their hearts. They respected her feelings well enough to part with the child they themselves so desperately wanted. But what else was to be done with a little girl who cried daily and starved herself? They had not expected her resistance and sorrow to be so deep-seated, with no sign of abatement after three months. It was better she return to her sister in Saskatchewan. Unwilling or absolutely incapable of giving her new life a chance, of allowing herself to grow into the strange landscape and get used to the new family, refusing to accustom herself, as children inevitably did, to loss and separation, paying a price in psychological and emotional consequences, Annie greeted the news of her eventual return to Dysart in a kind of trance. Her skeptical habit of mind perhaps originated ironically in receiving good news. How could she believe that her fondest wish would come true when her wishes thus far had perished like the fields of wheat in a prairie fire?

When the black car returned—always a black car in her memory—she had expected to see her brother Nick, assuming he shared her feelings of dislocation and dismay. He may well have done so, but he did not share the return journey home. It would be years before she saw her brother again, but the knowledge that Tenka would rush out of the house and greet her with loving arms mitigated that sorrow. The car carried her uncle Simeon, grudgingly come down from Saskatchewan to retrieve the thankless child. Her foster parents gave her a box of sandwiches and cookies, she remembered, and they embraced her in a farewell hug. Still wary and now distrustful of good news, for the world could break in two in a moment and love could be snatched away like a rabbit gripped by a hawk and hoisted in flight to meet its eventual death. Uncle Simeon spoke very little on the way back, nor did she think to ask where Tenka was. She could sense that he wasn't particularly happy to see her; the cost and inconvenience of the trip, as well as his dismay over a problem thought solved, were apparent in his refusal to speak. But Annie could tolerate Uncle's sullen anger. She wasn't going to live with him. In her childish fancy, she assumed she was returning to her father's farm to reconstruct the lost life of her childhood with her family, and she found solace in this wishful thinking.

CHAPTER 9

Beads about the neck
and the Devil in the heart.

The journeys from Dysart to Montana and back again would not ordinarily present a major shock to one's cultural sensitivities, the landscape foreign, not alien, but the journeys absolutely split Annie's sense of self and security. Some children survived being shunted back and forth in the midst of great sorrow without psychological harm; others did not. On the verge of a nervous breakdown, although that term was rarely applied to children, during her brief stay in Helena, where grief found no familiar people or patterns to restrain it, Annie worked herself up into a state of near hysteria. The bewildered couple regretted their decision to take Annie into their home, although they had tried hard to understand and console. That she was relieved to return home did not mitigate her profound experience of loss and separation.

Having been torn away from her father's farm, she clung to her hopelessly idealized conception of home all the more on her return. Hence, her desire to travel as an adult directly conflicted with her craving for stability and her discomfort in the presence of strangers. As impatience combined with rage and sorrow, Annie's heart and memory transfigured her father, rendering him superior in death to what he could possibly have been in life.

It was settled among those who made the decision regarding Annie's life that, ungrateful as she was in a foster home south of the border, she had to learn gratitude and self-control north of the forty-ninth parallel in her aunt's house. Hindsight always provides flawless vision. Several households could have found room for Samson's child. Her maternal grandparents could have taken her in, although they had made it clear that Nick was the limit of their compassion. Her uncle Simeon and aunt Eudora had opened their door to Annie's brother John. When he ran away, thankless child, they shut the door behind him. Still, one relative stepped forward out of the crowd of her own domestic circumstances to offer a home to her brother's child.

It was a serious error of judgment to place a child like Annie in a household where many children already lived in too few rooms, run by a woman full of strange contradictions and hostilities. Built by her prospering husband, Tudor, whose fortunes increased during the twenties when crops were abundant and prices reasonably high, Sophie's house had three bedrooms with gables on the second floor under its pitched roof. The pride of any Romanian immigrant woman, the kitchen boasted a new white McClary stove; the good parlour, used only for special occasions, a horsehair-stuffed settee, icons carried over the Atlantic and a dish cupboard with glass doors. On completion the house had been blessed by the priest himself and would be at the beginning of each New Year, as was the custom. Small, but architecturally well proportioned, it stood handsomely in the midst of farm buildings such as the smokehouse, tackle shed, poultry house, a stable, barns and the summer kitchen with its wood-burning stove and water pump.

An extensive vegetable patch behind the house, Sophie's special pride and joy, was the envy of her neighbours. Enriched with well-aged manure, always plentiful in supply, the garden that Sophie assiduously cultivated like a nun at her devotions provided sufficient leaf and root crops to feed the entire family. No one grew cabbages like Sophie, or bell peppers, the latter no mean achievement in a land with a relatively short growing season and early frosts. A short but hefty woman, round-faced and stern in countenance, broad bosomed and shouldered as Romanian peasant women tend to get, a voice like "a cow in labour," to quote my mother, she must have been attractive at one time in her own way. Sophie had enjoyed her share of suitors as a young woman. Her marriage, though, may have been a matter of arrangement between respective families, a still-common practice in those days. Young people met at church or at other social functions, their parents eyed each other, nodded approval and pursued matters from there.

Married at sixteen to a farmer, illiterate and intellectually incurious, utterly unfamiliar with the world outside of her Romanian farm and village where she had lived until her own family immigrated, producing a baby every year or two, Sophie viciously loathed the very idea of my mother. Despite the prosaic details of her successful rural existence, despite her maternity and prosperity, despite her own perfectly contented children, Sophie resented Annie's existence. Her sense of family perhaps compelled Sophie to take Annie into her house, but she despised the girl's intelligence, which manifested itself with frightening rapidity once Annie began participating in the household chores, going to school and engaging in shouting matches with her aunt.

Sophie distrusted Annie's dark looks, darker than most, suspiciously Gypsy- or Turkish-looking, and blamed her unaccountably for the death of both Rahila and Samson. *Cioară, cioară, cioară*, damned crow, evil crow, Devil's child, filth and wastrel, cow dung and chickenshit, greedy and thankless: whatever abuse came to mind, Sophie hurled at my mother; whatever instrument came to hand, Sophie applied to my mother's body. John, more fortunate than Annie insofar as he escaped physical and psychological brutality, would spend the rest of his life wandering from place to place. Annie seemingly enjoyed the benefits of a settled environment, although her sense of homelessness was equal to her brother's. But she knew what her duty was from day to day, where she was expected to be, what she was expected to do.

Dedication, however, did not deflect abuse. Annie's knowledge and competence, quickly developing into domestic expertise that put Sophie's to shame, intensified her aunt's attacks. The repeated assaults, although not breaking Annie's ability to resist, weakened her sense of belonging. Annie was in danger of becoming dislocated like her brother John. Each slap across the side of the head, each whip of the belt, each blow of the broomstick, every night spent in cow stalls: ceaseless reminders that however loving and settled the house, it wasn't Annie's home and she did not belong. *Nu face doi bani*: Sophie repeatedly called Annie worthless over the years, and the damage was inevitably done.

Surrounded by her own happy children, well clothed and well fed, speaking always of her dear departed brother and his unfortunate children, Sophie never insulted Annie's brothers or sisters. Not even Sophie knew how shockingly capable she was of harming a child until Annie crossed her threshold. Some of her reactions to my mother could well be attributed to darker, barbaric aspects of the human mind, not yet refined out of existence. Pogroms never lacked for perpetrators. Love of God, compromised by fear of the Devil, aroused blood lust in one form or another. Brutality, whether in the untutored or sophisticated heart, needs an object.

On the other hand, to be fair, Sophie worked from pre-dawn to well past the riding of the moon over the sky. Exhaustion and frustration expressed themselves in anger and abuse, with Annie providing the necessary means. In a household where patriarchal authority acquired the immutability of codes carved in stone, a woman's sense of oppression could easily be inflicted on a scape-goat. My mother tried to convince herself that the woman was mad, but many children are beaten within an inch of life by clinically sane people often quoting the Bible as justification. Sophie was religious. She stood in the church, adored by her brood of children, respected by the community, candle in a hand still red and sore from all the slapping administered that morning to her niece, who was not allowed to attend church that day because she had burned the *colivă*, singing the responses and crossing herself as often and devoutly as the next woman. How she could pray and slap her niece senseless, my mother could never figure out. As a consequence, Annie developed a profound skepticism toward people who confused church attendance with goodness.

My mother had scant memory of her uncle Tudor, Sophie's husband, because he, too, believed raising children was exclusively a woman's domain. If she also worked in the fields, in the gardens, in the poultry house, like most of the women, that labour did not necessarily lessen her responsibilities in the house. Annie said little about her uncle because he had nothing to do with her life. He was trudging or riding a tractor in the fields, ploughing or harvesting, herding or slaughtering, driving grain to the elevators in town or meeting with other men to discuss whatever agricultural policy impinged on their lives. Unlike her own father, Uncle Tudor neither danced nor played a musical instrument. If he swung his children in the air the way Samson had that magnificent christening day, Annie had never seen it. He left the house, his boots pulled on, cap on his head, before the sun rose and returned in time for supper as it set. In the winter he passed most of the day working in the tackle shed or attending all-male activities in Dysart or Cupar or Lipton with other farmers. Served first at supper, he ate silently, then withdrew from the table and went about his business in another room. Annie remembered Sophie getting up from the table to wipe her husband's fingers after he had eaten spareribs. She swore she would never do the same, and she never did.

When it came to raising children, Sophie and Tudor lived a parallel existence. Whatever Sophie chose to do, especially with a child who was not even related to him by blood, was not a matter with which Annie's uncle concerned himself. Even though he disciplined his own children with his own hand or belt at Sophie's behest—not a frequent occurrence, as the misdeeds of her children could often be blamed on Annie—Tudor left the application of brutality to her own devising. Of all the stories I heard growing up, the stories of Aunt Sophie and her wickedness tumbled out of my mother's mouth like toads and vipers. That she might have blighted her own son's childhood by describing the misery of hers seemed not to have occurred to her.

When Annie returned to Dysart in 1921 or 1922, the main street was essentially a rutted dirt road, incredibly dusty during the hot dry summers, muddy and difficult to negotiate by foot or wheel during spring runoff time and heavy rains. The one- and two-storey wood buildings never obscured the sky, an ever-dramatic, expansive presence. Entering the town was like arriving at the end of the world, where the immensity of unstructured space nullified the human lives, and the unending demands of weather and agriculture forbid larger pursuits of civilization.

Not so long ago her own father had lived in a land broken and mended, devastated and repeatedly rebuilt over a two-thousand-year history, a land trod upon by Roman legions and blessed by Byzantine bishops. Ravaged by succeeding invaders from the old Turks to German soldiers who, during the last days of the First World War, like Napoleon's army retreating from Holy Mother

Russia, stole whatever they could collect in a thieving rampage, the territories and provinces of old Romania were still very much the domains of churches and monasteries, peasants and landlords, saints and devils, forests and mountains, bears and wolves. The Western-leaning, civilized culture of Transylvania has not withstood the Hollywood stereotypes of sinister counts, Gypsy women, werewolves and vampires. Images of this ancient culture, like artifacts in a museum case, influenced Annie's imagination all her life. Contrary to her long-held desire, she never visited Transylvania. What she hadn't seen could always remain mythical and magical, a prevalent tendency in the peasant mind.

Daydreaming in the middle of a dirt road in an early Canadian prairie town, not a tree in sight, under the blue bowl of the sky, the child Annie neither stared into vacancy nor, like a mystic, apprehended the presence of divinity. She peered into the great distance between the reality of her bruised body and the dream of her escape. Railway tracks, more tangible than the mythical bird of Romania, always led somewhere. Paradoxically, she had already been taken somewhere, if not by train, then by car, only to discover that change of place did not in fact offer a change of heart.

Three churches and three graveyards, the former empty for longer and longer periods of time, the latter reaching full capacity. Attendance at church, especially the Orthodox *biserică*, has inevitably declined. The world my mother inhabited no longer exists except in personal stories, fragments of memories, residual rites and ceremonies, lonely, abandoned farm buildings leaning to the point of collapse and a Byzantine church that is now a heritage site. Everything that shaped and influenced her childhood and early youth, church and school, is now a museum, the people all dead. The educational system achieving its purpose, the immigrants, Romanians and other groups, eventually blended into the mainstream or departed, the assimilation and diaspora as much psychological as cultural, now more or less complete.

Also a museum of sorts, her aunt's house of the 1920s still stands, along with other farm buildings, on its quarter section of land not far from Dysart, several miles from Samson's farm. Two floors high, weather-beaten grey wood, as virtually all the prairie ruins are, its windows boarded up, a foundation built of stones dug up from the fields, it is as unlike a traditional Romanian peasant house as can be except for the surprisingly ornate carved lintel above the front door, perhaps a deliberate architectural reminder of ancestral origins or nostalgia carved into wood. The land, not stereotypically flat in this part of Saskatchewan, is divided into rolling and dipping fields, broken by a coulee behind the house where Annie used to hide and play. The house was built on the highest knoll of the landscape, and from the kitchen door, the circular, brown-edged signs of a dried-up slough are visible in the distance.

My mother had a tendency to stare into space or drop her head and stop crocheting as if overtaken by fatigue, but she was really overtaken by an enormous sense of confinement, which all the work of her daily life could not obliterate. Fighting off incipient depression, she often began telling another story, the art of narrative clearly becoming a kind of panacea and purge. A mother's moods are often inconvenient for her children, so they tend to ignore them. Standing on the knoll outside her aunt's kitchen, she once told me, distance forever leading her imagination outward, sky untrammelled by cluttered, urban landscape, my mother clearly saw the possibility of exit. The immeasurable distance beckoned her. One day she would place the distance like a shield between herself and the woman with the ponderous breasts, screaming in the kitchen at her to use the clothes mangle and wring out the dripping-wet laundry. Hanging clothes to dry was neither a burden nor a punishment because it led Annie outside, within view of the burgeoning vegetables and the consolation she derived from seedlings and sky.

The first home of the first Romanian farmers in the Saskatchewan prairies was a hole in the ground, *bourdeas* in Romanian, more accurately meaning a hole or cave in the side of a hill, a reminder of the hilly terrain of parts of Romania. In his sod hut, Samson did not define his future by the nature of his residence, nor did anyone else who moved to Saskatchewan huddle for long in a hole and let the world go by. The point of immigration to the prairies was to create a new world, not to hide from it. Annie always spoke warmly about her first home, able to transform mud into a pre-lapsarian paradise where she was loved and where flowers blossomed in the walls.

In 1911, a literary and dramatic society was formed in the town of Cupar, a few miles away. Immortalized in Pauline Johnson's poem "Legend of Qu'Appelle," the town of Fort Qu'Appelle was a vibrant and flourishing community, with some pretensions to grandeur. Across the street from the Hudson's Bay store, Dunk the Druggist proudly advertised drugs, candies and cigars for sale. Still largely under the influence of the town's English immigrants, cricket, tennis, polo and bicycle clubs, the latter as early as 1902, had little trouble finding members. A junior hockey team played in 1918. There was, of course, a Chinese laundry, Low Kee's, opened in 1913. A tuberculosis sanatorium was built, and as the disease was still virulent, it was filled to capacity in these years. Elegant homes rose on the shores of the lakes of the valley. The Fort Hotel was built in 1913, a substantial stone structure very well patronized by well-to-do Regina visitors and tourists.

Also within hailing distance of Dysart, Saskatchewan's first minister of agriculture, William Motherwell, with his wife, Adeline Rogers, combined agricultural necessities and civilized

amenities in their homestead and experimental farm at Aber-
nethy. A fieldstone house, the latest in agricultural technology, a
private phone line, books and music and a barn (now also a heritage site) whose ceiling network of beams astonishingly reminds
one of a Gothic cathedral, the Motherwell Homestead itself cor-
rects any notion that the Saskatchewan region where Annie lived
as a child was an isolated and soul-destroying wasteland. In a matter of a decade, different and opposing levels of sophistication
and technology operated one next to the other, an anglophile
neighbour reading Shakespeare next to an illiterate European
peasant who spoke no English; his gasoline-and-kerosene two-
cylinder opposed-motor Avery tractor noisily turning the soil in
the field opposite two oxen dragging a hand-held plough. Children of the well-to-do dressed in suits and lace, going all the way
through primary and secondary schools, sometimes private, and
finishing their education in England. They lived a few miles down
the way from Annie, who played in bare feet in a public schoolyard, spoke a mixture of perfect Romanian and broken English,
happy to learn, until her aunt Sophie snatched her out of the
classroom, shattering her love of learning like the eggs of a prairie
grouse under the heavy trudge of the ox.

CHAPTER 10

*It is not with saying honey
that sweetness will come to the mouth.*

Within the oldest Romanian Orthodox community in Canada,
English-language schools raised Annie out of the intellectual
limitations of her narrow and frustrated life. They offered
through the subject matter of their curriculum alternative
visions, some more plausible than others, but all so unlike
Annie's own daily life as clouds are to clods of earth. The
Saskatchewan public school system developed rapidly in the first
decades of the twentieth century, each family inscribing its name
on the rolls and sending its children to a specific school district.
Annie attended at least two of the Dysart-region schools, one
near her early childhood home and the other close to her later
home. Her liking of school, especially after her return to Dysart,
grew in direct proportion to her loathing of her aunt's house.
Despite all the rules and regulations of behaviour and deportment, the teacher's pointer and the leather strap, the very otherworldliness of the school room, smelling of tung and kerosene
oil, fed into Annie's imagination like an underground stream.
She became aware of the existence of worlds so unlike her own
that, warmed by the conventional Quebec heater in winter,
school offered unexpected attractions and stimulation of a sort
inconceivable in Mătuşă Sophie's house.

With so many children from different ethnic backgrounds,

only a few of whom were English, Romanians for a time forming the majority, the teachers entered a strenuous and paradoxical arena where they conducted classes based on a startlingly sophisticated but very anglo-centred curriculum. Born into families with little tradition of education, some fear and suspicion of the enlightened mind, few, if any, books present in their homes, physical strength and agricultural skill more important than history and literature, most of the children had no models of the intellectual life to emulate, certainly true in Annie's instance. Many of them were the first members of their family to attend any kind of school at all. Yet the collective belief of their parents that education in English was imperative in the new land, if only to learn basic literacy, bears witness to a tremendous desire to break from the ignorance of the past in the old countries. Not everyone, of course, recognized the virtue of education, Aunt Sophie being one of them.

Annie had always been receptive to stories, although reading in English would pose problems and her development was slow at the beginning. The kind of stories she knew had been conveyed by means of the body, of the mouth, of music and gestures. When telling a story, Samson had sometimes slipped into chants and veered into songs, stamped his feet and clapped his hands above his head, growled like a brown bear in the Carpathians, or barked like a fox, or hooted like an owl, or bent his body forward, curving his back like a scythe, twisting his hands and changing his voice so he sounded like the Russian witch Baba Yaga, stories of whom he had learned himself as a child. At school the teacher told the children to sit still and listen as she read a story out of Andrew Lang's *Blue Fairy Book*.

Trying to control her feet and hands while listening to a story of children lost in the forest, their trail of crumbs picked up by birds, the seemingly loving woman with the house of food inviting the children to eat and eat: how was it possible to sit still when she remembered her own father telling the same story or one very similar to it? Annie was unable to understand the meaning of being lost in a forest when she lived in a land unblocked by trees. Her memory of the Montana landscape was beginning to fade. With no hidden and devious pathways in a land where she could see a tractor in the field until it disappeared miles away on the horizon, the only approximation to forest being the bushes, aspens and Manitoba maples of the coulees (and you only had to climb up to see where you were), Annie relied on the images of her father's stories to give her a sense of great and terrifying darkness in which quasi-demonic creatures lurked. Becoming the characters he described, Tată would make his voice stern and forbidding like the cold-hearted, false mother who ordered her husband to abandon the children in the woods. Then it became kindly and croaking when he invited the children to eat the windowsill made of cheese *plăcintă* or to lick the marzipan panes of the windows.

How little she had eaten on many a morning, her eagerness to rush out of her aunt's house so strong that she dressed hurriedly after setting the table and helping to prepare the breakfast, snatching food unless forced to sit with aunt's several children, threatened by one implement or another if she did not obey, and escaped before her aunt could haul her back into the house. It didn't matter if she endured punishment later in the day on returning home. Rushing to attend school at the risk of a severe beating with a belt or broomstick may attest to an all-consuming desire for knowledge, but Annie was motivated as much by hatred of her *mătuşă* as she was by love of education.

In the two-room school, she sat on a bench nailed to the floor, staring at a map of the Dominion of Canada on the wall. She could never comprehend the size of the country, an impossible task anyway, the minuscule point where she resided not even marked, as if no one existed in the spaces the map did not acknowledge by name. Next to the map of Canada hung the map of the world, showing the great body of water over which her parents had sailed, greater in size than all the lakes and ponds and sloughs of Saskatchewan poured together into one gigantic basin. Sometimes, turning to look out the window at the racing streaks of clouds blown by the forever wind like white ribbons across the blue of the sky, she tried to imagine how it was possible to leave Dysart and travel to the ends of the map to places called Newfoundland and Baffin Island and Tierra del Fuego and Australia. She had already been taken away to another country, and the experience had terrified her, had increased her sense of vulnerability and defencelessness.

She didn't want to go away when she lived with her father, brothers and sisters. But her father had died and she had been separated from her brothers and sisters. Here she was sitting in a school room, staring at the sky, the spaces left in her heart by the disappearance of her family greater than all the spaces on the maps. Called to attention by the teacher's smacking a pointer on her desk, startled out of reverie and incipient self-pity, Annie dipped her pen nib into the inkwell, but it slipped and rolled to the floor. She was thankful for having to inscribe a hundred times "I will pay attention" in her notebook without spilling blobs of blue ink over the letters—writing with a straight pen requires a disciplined and patient hand—for she could bow her head and hide the tears.

The first time Annie saw the geographic shape and location of Romania, a country whose borders shrank and grew from one century to the next, she remembered the name of the place her father had left, although it was too small to be identified on the map. Her experience of Montana notwithstanding, she tried to visualize what his life must have been like in the valleys between the misty blue, heavily forested mountain ranges. Without a concrete experience of the world, without a sense of distance and its relationship to time, she could not begin to imagine how far away Romania was. On that very first day she became aware of Romania on the map, Annie promised herself that she would travel back to her father's homeland, in a sense her own homeland as well. Even though she didn't want to leave home or be taken away, she believed that one day she would walk the streets of her father's village and hike up the mountains covered in mist and legends.

Whenever she listened to a story that was vaguely familiar to her (her teachers tended to read aloud, probably to improve their students' comprehension of spoken English rather than to convey the joy of narrative, for it's a rare teacher who loves literature more than lessons), Annie recovered her lapsed attention and, riveted, followed the story to the end. Because the curriculum of the day was so rich in literary narratives, and because of her father's theatrical and physical presentations of stories, Annie developed a keen sense of drama and telling detail when she narrated her own stories in later life, using, like Samson, her hands and voice to convey character and meaning.

Keeping farm children in schools was no easy task as so many, the boys especially, tended to drop classes according to the dictates of agricultural seasons and the demands of the farm. Maps and lessons and stories did not appeal to every student. Annie's brother John, incapable of sitting still for long and incapable of focusing on abstractions, would not stay in school as long as his sister, who herself did not reach the end of Grade 8. It always remained a source of resentment, embarrassment and profound regret for Annie that she had never been allowed to complete her public school studies, although she liked to boast that she knew more than her husband. But for the few years she attended, Annie became emotionally and intellectually engaged in her studies. Once her English developed to the point of functional literacy, she learned quickly. To some degree her memories of schooling became another form of the suppositional thinking to which she was especially prone. If she could only have stayed in school; if her aunt had not been so cruel; if her father had lived, he would have encouraged and supported her studies: the refrain was often heard. My mother believed that she had been deliberately deprived of further education, "robbed of school," to quote her phrase. Hungering for education, she felt forever famished.

The Dysart school Annie attended was built in 1917 and still stands, much larger and more imposing today than it was when she was a student, now a heritage museum for the town, unremarkable architecturally but memorable historically. So many children of recent immigrants struggled with an English curriculum that puts contemporary public school curriculums to shame. It's astonishing to think Annie and other Romanian children could well have been expected to read and understand *King Lear* in a prose version and *Beowulf*, not to mention sections from Homer, all contained in the two volumes of *Highroads to Literature* published by Nelson, or poems by Yeats, Kipling and Hardy in *Modern Poetry*, under the general editorship of the ubiquitous Sir Arthur Quiller-Couch. *The Alexandra Readers* series, published earlier in the century, introduced them to Dickens and Ben Jonson, Susanna Moodie and Pauline Johnson. *The Canadian Readers* series, Book V, published in 1928 after Annie had departed, contains Tennyson, Twain, Hawthorne and, closer to the events of the mid-nineteenth century than we are today, D'Arcy McGee. Arithmetic texts like *Individual Arithmetic: Book Four* taught the fundamentals and more, although Annie never felt entirely comfortable with numbers. Encyclopedias like the eight-volume set of the *Dominion Educator* were available on the classroom bookshelves. *The King Edward Music Reader* taught children the notation and language of music, and the Atlas School Supply company of Chicago may well have provided a giant relief map of the continents, one of which now hangs in the Indian Head schoolhouse, not far from Dysart.

Schooling was a means of smoothing out the rougher edges of ethnic differences, of assimilating the foreign child into the English mainstream, thereby weakening the ties to her own language and traditions. A reflection of British imperial interests and deficient in American and non-European histories, the curriculum provided substance for the young mind. A cornucopia of endless stories spilled into the classroom. They made more sense when the teacher or another student read them aloud than when Annie had to stand, horrifying experience, and read them herself, an exercise for which she never volunteered. Sensitive about her crooked teeth and incomplete grasp of English syntax, she developed the habit of concealing her mouth with her hand when she spoke in front of strangers. Self-conscious in the extreme, she hated the notion of being watched, a sensation she translated into being criticized. She began wishing herself invisible like the genie in the brass lamp in some of Tătă's stories. The desire to disappear later developed into feelings of unconnectedness, exacerbated by chronic depression, which she fought to deflect on a daily basis through the distracting and curative powers of work and family. Dedication to her responsibilities prevented crippling self-absorption.

The school sparked some hitherto untouched element in Annie's character: she took to her studies not with the dilatory resentment of many of her classmates, especially the boys, but with an astonishing eagerness. She flitted from page to page of the books in her impatience to consume their contents, however haphazardly, having to be called to focus on the specific lesson of the moment. That she possessed a remarkable intelligence cannot be disputed, not merely a capacity but the imagination for learning, a much greater gift. Without support or encouragement or, these crucial elements lacking, without even merciful indifference, her academic inclinations in that two-room schoolhouse on the Saskatchewan prairie sputtered and died. Circumstances of her childhood eventually overwhelmed and snuffed out potential. What Annie then lost, she never regained. Without a library, without books, without mentors, without models to follow, without means, without options, without family love and tolerance, she would have required superhuman effort to sustain an interest in school and develop her studies over a long period of time. As my mother was neither more nor less than human and subject to the laws of nature, her struggles as a child did not push her far academically. The spark of learning scarcely had a chance to burn. More seriously, she seemed to have lost the ability to rekindle the flame, not only because poverty and overwork—no friends to education—prevented much, but also because psychologically she could not rebuild what had been destroyed.

Like so many parents of her generation, Annie liked to remind her own children how she had to walk several miles to and from school, as though the lack of transportation indicated superior physical and emotional stamina. Perhaps it did. Strong legs and a well-tempered mind contribute to the success of any hike. In Annie's case, her aunt's home was almost three miles from the Dysart school, not a great distance for an adult to cover by foot in the spring, nor impossible on one of the prairie's blue-bright winter days, cold as the Devil's heart, my mother used to say.

One day, after clearing the breakfast table, which she, and none of the other children, had to do, and hurrying to get dressed for school, my mother looked for her shoes. Aunt Sophie wanted the child to remain home and help with the laundry. It was Monday, a dry wind was blowing across the sunny land, and the volume of sheets and clothes in a household of several people filled three baskets. Her own children she sent to school except for the two or three not yet of school age. Annie could also look after them. What difference did it make if she missed a day? This wasn't the first time Sophie had kept Annie out of school.

Proud of the shoes her Jewish parents in Montana had given her, Annie wore them, weather permitting, and walked to school as carefully as possible to avoid scuffing them. Resenting the fact that Annie not only attended school but actually desired to go, when she herself could scarcely read and write, the exasperated woman decided to block the child's way. Moreover, evidence suggests that Annie was brighter than Sophie's own children, that the girl's performance in school put those of hers in the shade. Making invidious comparisons, even Sophie could see that her children suffered in comparison with her niece, a motherless brat. Who would have thought that the dark little thing could be so smart, and her parents dead? It wasn't natural. Well, the Devil played all sorts of tricks on the unwary. What did it matter that Annie was smart, anyway? What good would an education do the orphaned girl? She should learn how to bake bread and pluck chickens and till the soil and sew pillowcases and make herself useful in a house where she really wasn't wanted.

Still very much a peasant woman with a mind more tenebrous and superstitious than enlightened and rational, never having attended school herself, Sophie paradoxically sent her own children for an education she could not even begin to understand while seeking to hobble Annie's aspirations. Jealousy and rage, so closely allied, assumed subtle guises and blatant forms. Sophie snatched the shoes out of Annie's hands, grabbed Annie by the hair, pushed her into the windowless pantry and locked the door, then hid them. My mother said it was like having her scalp lifted off her skull—she was sure droplets of blood sprinkled from the roots of her hair. The other children had already left for school. The child screamed among the crock pots, pounded the door, then cried until Sophie unlocked the door.

Annie frantically searched the house, hollering for her shoes up the stairs and down as if they could hear and respond. When she couldn't find them under her bed or in her box or under any of the other beds or in the one and only closet in the house or among the pile of boots kept outside the kitchen, even inside the McClary range, her aunt's delight, the oven still warm from the bread, Annie screamed even louder. She demanded that Sophie restore the shoes. Sophie assumed the stance of a bull in the field about to charge, my mother said, her broad bosom heaving, snorting, missing only the ring in the nose. A cleaver lay, ideal for hacking through bones, on the thick cutting board. Annie remembered all her life the sound it made when it whacked through the joints of meat and thudded against the wood.

She could see that Sophie's eyes followed hers. The child moved faster than the bull. Annie didn't recall what she was thinking at the time, but she said that her mind blackened, although she did not faint, and the kitchen exploded in a burst of white light. Annie reached for the cleaver, then, words scalding her tongue before spraying out of her mouth, she called her aunt for the first, not the last, time *vrăjitoare*. She spat out the word "witch" over and over, *vrăjitoare, vrăjitoare!* the cleaver hot in her hand, until Aunt Sophie, probably horrified as much by the profanity out of a child's mouth as by the cleaver in her hand, crossed herself several times and stepped backward, out of range.

So, without shoes, Annie slammed out the door and began

racing down the sloping driveway to the main road. Children in this region often attended school barefoot, if the season allowed, at least until school rules and regulations dictated other-wise, and Annie was no exception on this day. She wasn't ashamed of appearing barefoot in the classroom; she feared the permanent loss of her shoes. What Sophie took away, Annie did not expect to see again. The grid road passing in front of the farm met another road running parallel to the train tracks. For two miles or so that early June day, the dew reflecting light of the still-rising sun, Annie followed the railway ties, sometimes hopping from one to the other between the iron rails in her bare feet, the soles getting wet from the dew, watching the sky for-ever stretch high and away leading to the other side of the world, depicted on the school map. Her rage simmered, then quietened, and she pretended it was a soft ball that she threw in the air and watched disappear in the middle of a wheat field.

The grain was green beneath the blue sky. Annie's Romanian sense of colour deepened and intensified on the prairie. The haze-free light was so clear that she could almost see all the colours in the world merge one into the other like her water-colours in school. Ahead of her down the tracks the Dysart grain elevators rose like dark pillars scarcely attached to the earth. She kept them in sight, singing to herself, cleansed of the wrath against Aunt Sophie, not because she hated the woman any less but because she was outside, under the sky, feeling the sun's heat on the wooden ties, the warm slipperiness of the iron rails.

Like so many Canadians, Annie developed an acute conscious-ness of weather conditions. And she knelt between the ties, placed the side of her head on one of the rails to listen for the approach of a distant, very distant, train, the soft music of its reg-ular rhythm beating through the track. It sounded like the music of the *toacă*, the bell-board she remembered from the day of the great christening party when Tată had been alive and dancing and raising toasts of *bragă* to all the blessed babies received into the church that day. Then she stopped, standing in the middle of the track, perhaps halfway between her aunt's farm and the grain elevator, seeing as far as it was possible to see down the tracks that narrowed toward the horizon, where the world ended in a kind of hazy blur, shot through with the green, gold and blue: there, so far away at the other end, was a place she could go one day to escape Aunt Sophie.

She listened as she paused in later life and disappeared into a private world where she was listening to her past. To the sound of a prairie sky and landscape on a warm June day: the whisper of grain brushing by the breeze; the slither of field mice; the rustle of grouse; the buzz of flies and dragonflies; the whizzing of magpies and yellow-headed blackbirds over the sloughs; prairie dogs scuttling down their holes; and the sound of her own longing and regrets. For Annie, what had passed in historical time remained fixed in her emotional present. The sounds of the past, like the sound of the invisible, distant train on the track, were always approaching behind her back. She gathered late-spring flowers to give to her teacher, knowing she could well be disciplined for being late again, but what did it matter?

She wouldn't tell the teacher about her hidden shoes. The soles of her feet had turned reddish purple, she remembered, like the painted daisy, and later they would blister. She never wore those shoes again, seeing them on the feet of one of her aunt's children about the same age and size as she. Her heart was broken again, Annie said, although she wished no harm on her cousin. To console herself for their loss, she fancied that she had given them to her cousin as a gift. The Dysart elevators reared high, enormous pillars, and the school was not so far away now. Throughout the decades, she still remembered pausing that day in front of a small shingled house on one of Dysart's few streets and watching an old woman dressed completely in black, her head covered with a black kerchief, kneeling and singing in front of a rose bush surrounded by white-painted stones. Annie vaguely remembered seeing the woman before but knew nothing about her. Her face was so lined and ridged with wrinkles that the child thought she was a hundred years old.

Too early for blossoms, the bush, having miraculously survived the harsh winter, looked large and vigorous to Annie, who was already developing an eye for such things. Every day after she planted her seeds in the vegetable garden, she would walk the rows looking for the first signs of life. She didn't recall ever noticing the bush in bloom, but she believed the roses must have been red, a colour and flower much loved by Romanians. The rose was my mother's favourite flower. The woman sang in a language Annie did not understand, possibly Hungarian or German, a kind of lullaby, it seemed to Annie, as if the rose bush were a baby cradled among the stones. When the old woman noticed my mother, she stood up, smiled and waved toward the front door as if inviting Annie into the yard. My mother said she wanted to accept the invitation, knowing food would probably be offered, for no one in Dysart asked you into a house without offering a plate of something delicious to eat. She wanted to ask about the rose bush. It seemed important to Annie that she understand its mystery. What had caused it to grow so large and bushy? How many flowers did it produce? What was the woman digging into the soil around the base? Did the singing help like magical words spilled into the ground, fertilizing the soil? But school awaited.

Just a pause by the fence, a thought or two about roses, and she was no longer angry with her aunt. All the way to school, keeping the line of tracks in sight, knowing they led so far away that the *vrăjitoare* would never be able to catch her, Annie hummed and skipped and remembered the story of *The Goose Girl*, how the poor princess was recognized in the end, and the treacherous servant girl was stuffed in a lidded barrel studded with nails and dragged through the streets by galloping horses.

CHAPTER 11

Fields have eyes, woods have ears.

Great Romanian peasant cooking of the past was labour-intensive—don't let anyone persuade you otherwise—which is why so many of the dishes and recipes are disappearing from the staple diet of a Romanian household. Moreover, the food is not politically correct, nutritionally speaking. Lard, butter, sugar, heavy creams and many eggs have now all been proscribed. Romanians of my mother's background and generation were not famous for their fat-free diets and low-cholesterol salads. Moreover, a Romanian portion is not a sliver, a slip, a spoonful, a demitasse or just a taste. *Plăcintă*, if properly laden with baked apple slices, dollops of butter and showers of spice, should dribble between the fingers as you raise a hand-sized piece, still steaming, to the lips. Cheese *plăcintă*, less slippery and redolent, but no less tantalizing, designed to add bulk to the hips, is also, or should be, served in great wedges. To eat sparingly at a Romanian table insults the cook; to serve stingily insults the guests and embarrasses the family, unless poverty has dictated otherwise. Even when poor, my mother could concoct a feast, if not fit for the Queen, at least filling to the stomach. For Romanians, generosity of spirit and celebration of life were always expressed through food, the love of family and friends mixed like cream in savoury soups and stews.

My mother learned to bake *plăcintă* and to prepare other Romanian dishes in Aunt Sophie's kitchen. Cutting lard or butter into flour strengthens the arms. Necessary, if one is going to wallop a child for proceeding too slowly. Aunt Sophie, with more heft than heart, possessed a very strong arm. The difficulty with *plăcintă*, though, is not the initial mixing of flour and grease in whatever form, although olive oil in place of lard or butter is not advisable. Where pigs, chickens and cows are slaughtered for meat, animal fat, the stuff of lard, quickly fills a pail. There was, of course, the romance of the butter churn, although the churning itself was laborious, not romantic. Designed to wring out the laundry, the clothes mangle was secured to a metal washing tub that also served as a churn in this and some other households. Butter churning wasn't a daily activity. The tendency was to eat bread, serviceable for soups and stews, without spreading a coat of butter on the slices, butter being reserved for other purposes. My mother often cut homemade bread by holding it against her hip within the crook of her elbow and slicing chunks off.

The specific difficulty with *plăcintă* resides in rolling, stretching and, miracle of culinary adroitness, folding the dough in such a way as to avoid splitting. The dough must be stretched over the surface of the table as thinly as possible, thin like a spider's web, thin like a cat's whisker, thin like a dragonfly's wing, which is to say very thin, indeed. *Plăcintă*, or strudel to use a more familiar term, is neither a pie nor a bun. In fineness lies pleasure. If you can't see the lifeline on your palm beneath the dough, my mother used to say before she gave up Romanian cooking altogether, you haven't stretched it far enough.

Not an easy task. Consider a wooden table five feet by three and a half feet, usually covered over with oilcloth for the occasion or a taut, very clean bedsheet pinned under and around the legs of the table. That's almost eighteen square feet of surface to cover with a silky thin layer of dough, now resting in a mound in a brown crockery bowl. You start by flattening the dough a bit with the palm of your hand, then continue with a wooden rolling pin, like the kind Aunt Sophie kept in her kitchen. Rolling pins are serviceable. A handy weapon, they leave a terrific bruise on the upper arms or thighs. Quite wearying to the shoulders, the task of rolling out dough is still tricky. A child of ten or eleven, although she can do it, does it slowly, with pauses to wipe her brow with flour-spattered fingertips, time to catch her breath because she has been pushing too hard. Rolling is rhythm, a dance of the upper body and arms, not mere pushing like Sisyphus struggling uphill with a boulder. It takes time to become a chef, and considerable physical effort and strength.

Think of a pond, my mother used to say, a stone thrown in the middle and all the little waves in circles beginning from the point of the stone's plunk gently washing toward the cattails, something she had done in the sloughs of her childhood. Roll from the centre outward in all directions with the upper body, not just with the wrists. Positioning is everything. If the little girl is too short, her arms cannot provide sufficient angle and pressure on the pin, and the dough tends to become lumpy in its stretch, uneven in its thickness. In this case, the pin can be removed from her hands and whacked across the back of her legs. Hard enough to cause pain and bruising, not hard enough to cause the child to collapse—not yet, at any rate, for the dough remained to be stretched. So the child waited until the pain, tearing at the back of her thigh muscles and ripping up toward her neck and head, subsided. If a tear spurted out of her brown eyes onto the dough, no matter, for moisture was good, and sometimes my mother sprinkled a bit of water, not much, over the dough, falling like raindrops between the dabs of butter.

Plăcintă requires concentration and, like the dough, great stretches of time. Interruptions annoy the chef and threaten the texture, for you don't want the dough to dry and crack in the hot kitchen. Morning is the best time to make *plăcintă*, after the children have been sent to school, after Tudor has left the house for his day's work, after Annie, kept home again from the school she loved so much, has cleared the table and washed the dishes, pumping water into the kettle, heating it on the stove and pouring it into the basin. Washing dishes, wearisome task, is no measure of brutality. My mother never complained. When she saw her cousin Eva, Sophie's nine-year-old daughter, leave the house that late October day, kissing her mother goodbye, for Sophie was affectionate toward her children, holding the hand of her two younger brothers, also of school age, Annie did not wish the children dead. She envied the girl's freedom to go to school, although Eva did not shine in class, but Annie loved her cousin anyway. Now Sophie was pregnant again, in her sixth month. She would give birth to three more during Annie's time there, or was it five? All the children had been born at home, with the aid of farm wives. Sophie had been lucky—so far none of the children had died in early infancy. Far from giving Sophie a rosy glow, pregnancy blotched her face, added weight to an already thickset body and shortened her temper.

Annie never projected her hatred of her aunt onto her cousins; in fact, she was extremely affectionate, or tried to be, with them. With so many infants, Sophie found Annie's presence, although despised, necessary. If Sophie's children occasionally tended to be standoffish, hesitant toward or wary of Annie's overtures, they had their mother as a model on which to base their behaviour. There were times, though, when Sophie's children forgot that they were supposed to despise or ignore Annie, and they all played together and cracked eggs at Eastertime. Even Sophie relented now and then, for the price of brutality is time-consuming vigilance, and not even Sophie had the time to make every waking moment of Annie's life in her house miserable. The two youngest children, a boy and a girl, Mustafa and Lena, had been fed and clothed for the morning and told to keep out of the way. They could play in the kitchen yard, within Sophie's range of vision, or stay upstairs, but under no circumstances be underfoot in the kitchen. Tell that to any child under the age of five when you are baking with cinnamon-spiced apples, and see what happens. It was also Annie's job to keep them out of the kitchen if they dared to appear.

Sophie's was not a modern kitchen, of course, which means that preparation and cooking of food was far more difficult than it is today. *Plăcintă* requires a steady oven temperature, difficult to achieve and maintain in a wood-burning range, even the latest model. Woe betide the person responsible for under-cooked roasts or overbaked bread, more crust than soft centre, the bottom blackened. Later, when electricity eased the burden of culinary excellence, my mother still preferred to make *plăcintă* in the morning in the autumn. The availability of good apples is one reason why, of course (her favourite being Spies, which she called cooking apples, somewhat sour at first bite), but cheese is not dependent on a fall harvest. The wood stove also heated the kitchen to the point of suffocation, so who would want to overheat a kitchen during the sometimes breathtakingly hot prairie summers?

It was a wise farmer who built a summer kitchen for his wife, sometimes an addition to the house in the form of a lean-to, more often than not, as is the case with Sophie's farm, a separate struc-ture, sufficient to keep out the rain and the insects, roomy enough to swing a rolling pin. One cooked, then carried the food into the house. There was an icebox to keep the perishable food cool, great blocks of ice often cut out of the sloughs in the winter and dragged up to the ice shed and covered with hay. There, melting slowly with the arrival of warm weather, the blocks provided enough ice to last until the following winter. Sloughs would freeze soon enough again in the fall, and the process was repeated. Smoking and salting, canning and curing preserved what could not be kept cold. My mother also learned how to can food in the home she hated, an involved skill that was important to learn well, for the potential of food poisoning always remained a risk if the job was not done properly. Botulism kills.

To prepare Annie for her future role as the wife of whatever farmer was foolish enough to marry the cast-off, Sophie was determined to teach the child sufficient skills. Annie's failure would be a reflection on her own expertise or lack of it. A Romanian woman who did not know how to cook—God forbid! There would be no end to the laughter behind her back and the clucking of tongues, would there? So Annie began again to roll out the dough on the table, her shoulders sore, but getting into the rhythm, spreading the dough from the centre outward. Sophie was busy peeling the apples, her bosom heaving as each apple was cored and sliced. Hurry, Annie, the apple pieces, hundreds of them, were beginning to turn brown. Lemon was not available to prevent that process. Not that way, this way! With a slap across the back of the head that cracked right through to Annie's eardrums, Sophie grabbed the rolling pin. This way, *cioară*, this way. To give her her due, Sophie could roll *plăcintă* out swiftly, adroitly, thinly, the way it should be done. Annie, having bitten her tongue under the force of the slap, tasted blood, watched. A woman who could drag a calf out of a cow's uterus did not know her own strength. Tears again threatened to slip out of Annie's eyes. If Sophie had stopped to check the oven, to see if the wood was burning and the heat reaching the desired temperature, Annie told me she would have pushed her aunt headfirst into the flames, let Aunt Sophie's greased hair catch fire, just like in the story she had heard at school.

She continued where Sophie left off and returned to the apples. Annie had asked if she could peel, core and slice the fruit instead of roll the dough, thinking one task easier than the other. Not necessarily so. Dozens of apples are needed to produce filling for two pans of strudel, for baking apples shrink and sink. A heap soon becomes a mere layer in the oven. Annie had to peel and core the apples without wasting the juicy flesh of the fruit, the peels later fed to the pigs. The secrets of household and culinary success are many, most learned from experience, not from books or theory. The best, most essential ingredient of a Romanian recipe wasn't often written down for Annie to consult.

The dough had been rolled, thin as skin, thin as candle smoke in the church, the edges pulled over all four sides of the table. Careful, don't tear, don't rip, don't shred: stupid, stupid, stupid girl. *Prost!* Worse than a cow, you are so stupid! *Prost!* A slap, a pummel with a fist, a wrench, a pounding against the back of the head, not once, not twice, three times, until Annie screamed. Crows filching chicken feed in the kitchen garden were startled, cawed and flapped away, but not far. Crows are not easily intimidated. Annie saw them through the window when her head twisted under the blows. Chickens were allowed to scratch among the vegetable rows after the seeds had germinated, savouring the insects their pecking could find, a form of pest control. Annie herself had planted the beet and carrot seeds in the spring. A tooth must have broken or the tongue been cut. She tasted more blood. As long as she could see the garden and work among the vegetables, she could withstand much. The idea of growth, the very texture and smell of the soil, seeds as precious as gold, the crispness of cabbage leaves against her fingers as she brushed or picked off the green cabbage worms, the heat of the prairie sun tanning her face, even the thought of the garden lying beneath the snow in winter like a dream: these things consoled in the midst of the pain Aunt Sophie inflicted.

Mustafa and Lena, smelling the spiced apples, hearing Annie cry, ran into the kitchen, but Annie, wiping her nose, said she had burned herself on the stove. They would each get a piece of *plăcintă*, still hot from the oven, if they would be good and go outside, not too far—she didn't want to wander about looking for them. Sophie repaired the damage to the edges of the dough, for the ends had to be lifted over the apples, then rolled; any rips and tears would allow all the juices and apple slices to leak and slip out. What a pan looked like when juice leaked out and baked on the bottom! Annie would never be able to get it clean again. She would rather run out of the house and play with the children, take them down the sides of the coulee looking for abandoned birds' nests or to the slough in the middle of the grain field, recently harvested, and watch the last of the ducks before they flew away for the winter. Rinse her bloody mouth out.

Her hair pulled back into a bun shaped like a small beaver's tail, greased flat under a mesh net sprinkled with gold dots, Sophie dropped dabs of butter on the fine dough. Holding the big bowl on her hip, she cast the apple slices all over the rolled-out dough, her bulging belly preventing her from pressing against the edge. Sophie cast the apples with the same motion of the arm that she employed with flinging feed to the chickens. Then she dug into a small crock pot filled with a mixture of cinnamon and sugar, flicked the spice over the apples. Not once had she used a measuring spoon. Experience conferred speed and an unerring sense of quantities without the aid of utensils.

In the deepest cultural sense, one measured by hand and feel, not by tools. Such knowledge is instinctual and folkloric, not arithmetical. It was always hard to learn from my mother how many cups or teaspoons of any ingredient were required. For a proper position and ease of endeavour, it's wise to get close to the dough, not to let the arms extend too far from the body before the hands reach the edges of the table. As if displaying an exquisite sheet of lace in her widespread arms, Sophie showed Annie how to raise one side of the dough and, with a gentle lift and lean over the table, how to create the first fold at the edges so it looked like a creamy white rope. First one side, then the other. Now you do it, stupid girl.

So encouraged, Annie trembled, sucked on her lower lip and swallowed blood, the back of her legs still throbbing from the blow of the rolling pin. She held her breath, her eyes glazed with tears, seeing the children return to the kitchen, Lena sucking her thumb, her own black hair covered with a red kerchief. Sophie had the habit of staring at her niece and narrowing her eyes, waiting. Annie spread her arms at the other end of the table, stepped closer, grabbed the corners of the dough and began lifting. Even as the dough rose and drooped like a bedsheet in the centre, Annie knew something was going wrong. Not that way, not that way, *prost! Prost! Prost!* This way. Sophie pushed Annie aside and, once again, transformed into a merchant of a Turkish bazaar, raised and displayed the fine silken cloth. With admirable ease and dexterity, she created the first perfect roll of apple slices at this end of the table. Now you do the side, stupid girl!

It's one thing to fold *plăcintă* dough from the narrow ends of the table, quite another from the length of its sides. Being a somewhat small child for her age, Annie had arms that did not reach the corners, which meant the dough beyond her reach would droop from her fingers like a chicken's wattle. The children remained in the kitchen door, their eyes hungry for the strudel, not concerned about Annie's competence. There was no help for it but to proceed, which she did as carefully as possible, knowing even as she raised the dough that it was beginning to tear at the corners and fall too much in the centre. Sophie said nothing. Stepping closer to the edge until her own apron touched the dough, Annie raised and rolled, the tears dripping silently and the dough sagging. When she hoisted and rolled, she created a muddle of wrinkled dough gathered in the centre like a wet sheet in the laundry basket.

Even before Sophie struck, my mother said she could feel the force of the blow and instinctively braced herself against the edge of the table. She didn't know what Sophie had used then, for it didn't feel like the heavy thud of the wooden rolling pin, more like sharp cracks against the back of her neck, her head, her legs. Fearing for her face, she dared not turn around. Perhaps a fly swatter. Flies are endemic on farms. They drove Sophie crazy if she saw them in the kitchen, rubbing their hindlegs on her *mămăligă*. She had not acquired any kind of perspective that recognized the inevitability of certain phenomena. She attacked the flies. And Annie. My mother could not stop herself from crying out, cries she hoped could be heard all over the farm, in the trees, in the fields. Who was there to come running to her aid? No such thing had ever happened before. She bent forward as the smacks stung her back and Sophie bellowed. She screamed at Mustafa and Lena to leave the kitchen and not to forget what happened to bad children.

Rage is energizing. Once the arm is raised in fury, it tends to take on a life of its own, and Sophie for unaccountable reasons, at least none that my mother could define, continued the attack until Annie's skin reddened and swelled and broke. For the handle of the fly swatter was twisted wire. Annie, weakened by shock and pain, fell forward onto the table, her arms spread out the way they should for proper lifting of the dough, her fingers sliding among the apples and spices as the cutting lashes continued, this time across her bare arms. Her tears mixed with the sugar and spice. How very wonderful the aroma in the midst of misery.

Then Sophie stopped, grabbed the kerchief and, wrenching Annie's hair in her stubby hand, hoisted the child off the unfolded strudel by the head, dragged her screaming by the hair out the kitchen door and all the way across the yard to the cowshed where three cows, milked that morning, chewed their cud in the stalls. Sophie threw Annie into a corner, where the child banged against the wood planks of a stall, raising her arms in the air as if to ask God to witness the trials she must endure. Sophie locked the door behind her. Annie knelt in the straw, in the dirt, crying and wiping her nose with the apron, her back and arms welted, swollen with bruises and laced with fine threads of blood.

It was very difficult to think, but she could still smell the sweet scent of spiced apples. She huddled in the straw and stared at the cow's pimply pink udder. Annie learned a great deal about cows. Released many hours later by a silent Eva after the family had eaten supper and enjoyed the *plăcintă*, Annie cleared the table and washed the dishes after the sun set, scarcely able to stand. Aunt Sophie had left a covered dish of *plăcintă* for Annie to eat after she had done the dishes. When Sophie wasn't looking, Annie took the plate outside, the miracle of strudel so tempting and appetizing that she wanted to sit on the stoop and slowly eat so it would last. Baking always assuaged her pain and sorrow, a comfort she would rely on to some degree in later life. She fed the dessert to the pigs. Rather than returning to the house, she found her way to the vegetable plot and stood at the edge. There, remembering the pleasures of planting, she dreamed about standing on her very own land one day, hoeing between rows and rows of her own cabbages and beets, green and red like giant jewels raised out of the prairie earth by her love and care.

CHAPTER 12

Two meals won't do any harm;
two beatings will.

With the passage of time and the shifting and clouding of her memories, Annie telescoped the winters of her childhood into one landscape of snow drifting as high as the thatched roof of her father's sod house. It didn't matter if one winter saw less accumulation of snow than another; she piled all the winters together into one great blizzard that blocked the windows and doors. Nothing compared in her memory or imagination to the snow of the Saskatchewan prairie. However deep the snow in the East, it always fell short of the snow in the West. Sometimes it snowed for days at a time, my mother said, although she collapsed time in her old age the way she conflated events. A blizzard of several consecutive days may in fact have been several storms over a period of three or four months. And she couldn't go to school, which, contrary to our expectations, struck my mother as a particular hardship. Here, she was clearly recalling life in her aunt's, not her father's, house. The domestic nightmare of Aunt Sophie's domain was underpinned by a sentimental fantasy, the lost kingdom of her father's farm.

The front and back doors of Samson's house opening inward rather than out, Tată had had to tunnel his way through or climb the ladder to the little boarded-up window cut into the wall just under the gable of the roof and crawl directly onto the surface of the snow. Annie remembered his legs kicking above her head in the kitchen. Once he was outside, the only visible landmarks were the chimney and the top half of the barn. As if confined inside a pearl, the sun was a yellowy grey smudge. The rest of the world had disappeared in a white haze. Soon the sun broke through its opaque prison and scattered hard light all over the land, oceanically covered with snow. When she went outside, silver pins and stars whorled before and hurt her eyes. The snow was whiter than sheets on the clothesline, with streams of blue, yellow and muted rose like veins beneath the skin. She never experienced a green Christmas until she moved to Ontario.

Too bundled up to frolic, she once sank down to her neck and had to be hoisted out by her brothers, who lay flat on the surface to prevent themselves from drowning in the snow. Every move required a dig first. Every step a trudge. Some farmers wore snowshoes, those marvellously appropriate footgear for surviving winter on foot. She had none. The cold temperatures, though, if the body was properly protected, did not penetrate the skin to lick around and tongue the very marrow of the bones. The East always suffered from invidious comparisons; the icy air of the prairie invigorated and enchanted rather than disgusted. Yes, cows and people froze to death, she often said, as if the landscape were littered with the blue, congealed corpses. But she never minded the dry cold in the West as much as she did the damp chill of the East. The image of a snowy Christmas is so inextricably ingrained in our culture that a rainy Christmas, common enough in various parts of the country, irritated and sent her into a fug of nostalgic regrets. What matter if Aunt Sophie beat her on Christmas Day? At least snow had fallen.

Traditional Christmas festivities for Romanians, more so generations ago on the prairies than today, covered a several-week period. Still close to their ancestral villages and modes of thought, my mother's family, including her aunt's, followed at least some of the customs, sacrificing others on the altar of expediency and distance. It was easier for choirs of children to sing Romanian carols from door to door in a Transylvanian village when all the doors stood within knocking distance than it was to travel the snow-covered acreage from one farmhouse to another in Saskatchewan. A complicated and contradictory event at the best of times, Christmas (*Crăciun*) in Aunt Sophie's house for my mother was a matter of walking not in deep snow but on thin ice, more glaze than thickness, like stepping on and crashing through the first layer of ice covering the sloughs. A holiday, or in this context holy day, also a misnomer since it lasts weeks, strains a housekeeper's nerves and reduces bare tolerance to the point of naked aggression. To say that Aunt Sophie exploded daily during the Christmas season, given my mother's stories, is to say the bull bucks when its genitals are tied. To be fair, preparations for festivities and feasts often fell into the woman's lap, and her work was increased tenfold. Having borne and suckled several children, by nature volatile and somewhat short-tempered, resentful of the orphan child in her care, Sophie would have reached her wit's end.

Although the Orthodox faithful were required to undergo a six-week fast before Christmas on January 6, depriving themselves of meat, eggs, fish and milk or any food derived from animals, a fury of food preparation nonetheless occupied much of the time for the women. Traditional dishes served at this time of the year had to be prepared, in addition to ordinary meals, and prepared in quantities to feed more than the family. By preparation, it's understood that all the recipes were baked, like the famous cakes, from scratch. No one bought processed or packaged food. Cleaning was also crucially important because the priest, if available, would arrive some days before Christmas itself to bless the house. And no woman wanted household dirt and disarray sanctified.

Annie at this time became especially useful, lessening Sophie's regret and rage because my mother helped in the kitchen, slopped the floors, dusted the icons. So could Sophie's older children, and Annie said they contributed to the general household purge of filth and preparation of food. What struck her as unfair, however, an injustice that rankled until her aunt's death, was that Sophie punished Annie for the errors and incompetence of her own children. My mother had the bruises to prove it. The whipping post had been taken indoors and transformed into a pale and dark child, terrified of putting too much salt in the stew or allowing the pork wrapped in pastry, a variety of "pigs in a blanket," to burn in the oven.

Before Christmas, hogs were slaughtered, hoisted up by their separated hind legs, secured, hooves tied by ropes or chains and dangled from a beam in the barn or possibly a convenient tree or a rack designed for the purpose. Throats cut and bellies slit, the carcasses dripped their blood into pails, an iron kettle over fire steaming with boiling water. Slaughtering, bleeding, scraping, butchering and curing took some time and were tasks relegated to her uncle. Tastier and more convenient for purposes of the oven and table, piglets could also be sliced opened, drained, gutted and baked, mouths stuffed with wizened apples, ears decorated with ribbons and acting as a centrepiece on the Christmas table. After several weeks of a meatless fast, pork enticed and satisfied the famished. Turkey did not become a mainstay of the Christmas feast until after cultural assimilation.

On St. Nicholas's Day, December 6, tradition said that the good saint brought small gifts to the younger children of the household. In 1924, my mother, especially in the eyes of an unsympathetic aunt, did not qualify. The night before, Annie had been instructed to clean and polish the shoes of all the other children—perhaps six or seven cousins by then, she had lost count—and arrange them in a neat row under the lace-covered window of the parlour. In the morning, the children, including the recently born baby who had arrived in November, would find a little present—perhaps candy or coloured chalk, a ball, a miniature castle constructed out of marzipan or a rhinestone hair clip. When my mother polished the shoes given to her by the kind Montana Jewish couple, she remembered holding them to her chest and trying not to cry. Aunt Sophie slapped her when she heard a whimper or saw a tear.

Annie didn't mind terribly that Eva now wore the shoes. Although they were now two years old, Eva had taken care and tried not to scuff them, wore them only on special occasions, even carried rather than wore them on her way to school to preserve the soles and protect the leather. The fact remained that they belonged to Annie, who owned nothing at all in the household. In a world where presents were relatively few and far between, where small items found in shoes aroused excitement and pleasure, signalling the beginning of the great festive time of the year, Annie had no shoes to put under the window. Her aunt expressly forbade her to include her down-at-the-heel scruffy things retrieved from a clothing bin in the church hall, deemed serviceable enough for a thankless child. That meant, of course, St. Nicholas would leave nothing for Annie, not the smallest present. When Sophie found a means to express pettiness, she did so with a vengeance.

Polishing the shoes under the curious and expectant eyes of her cousins who, threatened with the wooden spoon on their backside, were forbidden to help Annie, my mother remembered a Christmas in her father's house. The last St. Nicholas Day before his death, Samson had helped his children polish their shoes, singing carols with them, while Tinca, not particularly cheerful at the best of times, nonetheless hummed the tunes as she kneaded the dough for the morning's bread. The next day, even before the cold winter sun glinted above the horizon—she was only seven at the time—frost covering the windowpanes like lace coverlets, Annie and her brothers and sisters had discovered their ankle-high shoes filled with sweets purchased from the drugstore in Fort Qu'Appelle.

Her cousins were ordered to leave the room and go upstairs to bed. Her uncle was working in one of the sheds, possibly cleaning the horse tackle or polishing a tractor, tasks he undertook this time of the year. Sophie clattered in the kitchen, the shadows of the declining day long and blue over the hillocks and banks of snow outside. Annie said she had never felt more alone in her life than she did that very moment, sitting on the floor, the shoes on sheets of newspaper to prevent the blacking from staining the braided rug. Too alone to scream for Tenka as she had done in Montana, Tenka who was now living in Regina, too alone even for profitless tears. She tried to convince herself that, at eleven, she was too old for presents. But the same neglect had occurred the year before and the year before that. A small matter, of no great consequence, it would have appeared, except Annie had reached the age when she could recognize her aunt's utter malevolence directed exclusively toward her orphaned niece, and she struggled not to blame herself.

Indifference would have been a blessing, but Sophie's repeated assaults on the girl's body and spirit, the incessant demeaning of her character and feelings—*prost! cioară!*—had begun to corrode Annie's sense of self. Perhaps she was as worthless and unlovable as Aunt proclaimed daily. Yet, much despised, she still yearned for what she had lost—the comfort of being completely loved and protected—even though, my mother admitted, she understood perfectly that she had as much chance of being loved as the pig had of surviving the knife. She rubbed the brush over the shoes, her body folded over, the sun sinking and the night beginning to slide over the sky, the emptiness profound, as if that metaphoric stone in her heart had tumbled out of its chamber, leaving residual dust in the cavity.

The first whack across the side of the head wakened her from sleep. Holding her precious shoes to her chest, Annie had fallen into a doze under the window. The blow knocked her against the table, which shook and caused an icon to fall off its doily-covered surface. Made of wood, it did not break, but for all the moral horror expressed in Sophie's crossing herself, as if the Devil himself had fallen asleep on her braided rug, it might as well have broken. My mother remembered clearly the weapon Sophie used this time, a heavy wooden mixing spoon, more flattened than rounded at the spoon end, ideal for mixing sticky ingredients in a large bowl. Annie would herself use the same spoon at Eastertime. Almost two feet long, thick handled, designed to withstand an enormous amount of downward and circular pressure and to plough and stir through resistance, the spoon cracked like splintering wood on Annie's head, then on her shoulders. Rolling away to avoid Sophie's reach and escape the blows, for the woman tried to catch hold of Annie's hair, my mother pleaded, begged her aunt to stop. The spoon smacked against the thighs and neck and arms, the pain like fire on the reddening skin.

The moon peeked through the half-frosted window, and the brass lamp hanging from the middle of the ceiling, its light more dim than useful, smelled of oil. The heat from the kitchen seldom reached the parlour, which was kept closed most of the year and opened only on occasions, like Christmas and the priest's visit in three weeks. In a shawl and sweater, her hair forever tied up in a net or hidden under a kerchief in the style of married women, Sophie demanded that Annie sit still. Her aunt wanted her to sit still so she could beat her, my mother said, perhaps more shocked after all those years by the bizarre request than the beating itself. Out of Sophie's bosom popped the cross she wore, the crucified Christ engraved on its surface. For a moment Annie thought to yank the cross off her aunt's neck. She regretted not doing so.

She remembered that her uncle appeared in the door and stood, watching Sophie repeatedly whack his niece with the wooden spoon, but said nothing. If she had expected some relief from his presence, my mother was mistaken. Her crime: dozing over a chore, or falling asleep with her fabulous shoes clutched to her breast—one or both, what did it matter? Inflamed and enraged and warming to the task, Sophie did not stop thrashing. Annie's body was on fire, her face smeared with blood from the cut on her lip and from the streaming from her nose, her brain growing darker and more numb with each blow. Then, no longer able to scramble and roll out of reach, she huddled on the floor, wrapped her arms around her knees and lowered her head, too stunned with pain to resist any longer. Annie believed that she would be beaten to death until Sophie suddenly stopped, wiped the mixing spoon with her apron and left the room, shutting the door behind her. Annie remained semi-conscious and shivering in the cold parlour, staring at an icon at her feet, and all the shoes she had polished, sitting in a perfect row, untouched by the furor, waiting to be filled through the generosity of a saint.

What happened the next day Annie couldn't exactly remember, but she suspected she had to show and explain the welts and bruises to the other children. Sophie allowed her to stay in bed and not to attend church service that Sunday morning. Annie did not believe her aunt's decision originated in compassion for her niece's suffering or remorse over the attack as much as it did in self-preservation. What people did not see, they would not comment on. Her own children had been well instructed not to carry tales or divulge family business.

Eva understood that Annie had been beaten and wished her mother wouldn't do it, but maybe Annie should try harder not to be so difficult and to pay attention. Eva felt sorry for her cousin, but in defence of her own mother blamed Annie for Sophie's savagery. The swellings subsided, the cuts healed, the bruises faded, no bones were broken, and the house needed to be cleaned thoroughly and maintained in time for the blessing. The food had to be cooked, the chickens fed, the cows milked, the table scoured, the stove fired, the children washed, the laundry done: beating or no, her work waited. If she did not do it, then another beating. If she did not to it according to Sophie's specifications, then another beating. She began to remember days of the week on the basis of when a beating did or did not occur.

An old Romanian folk tale describes the sky separating, the heavens opening on New Year's night. For one brief and illuminating moment, too blinding to last longer, God Himself appears, divinity becomes visible, not in the symbolic form of an icon but in the indescribable face of the Creator of the universe. On New Year's Eve that Christmas season, my mother said she stared out the window after all the children had fallen asleep, looked up long and hard, for she believed then, and waited for God to appear before the faithful, prayed for God to show His merciful face. The prairie winter night spangled with stars above a land blanketed with blue-and-purple-tinged snow is as close to a metaphor for divinity as one can get, if one is so inclined.

My mother wasn't looking for a metaphor. With the fervent prayer of an abused and brutalized child, she looked toward God for the help she did not find on earth. The heavens, though, did not open like the door leading into the sanctuary behind the iconostasis in the church. The dark Saskatchewan sky did not separate to reveal such breathtaking peace and beauty, such blessed love and hope as would have instantly transformed and inspired her life. When telling this story, Annie pretended that she hadn't really expected to see God's face that night, but the regretful drop in her voice and a shift in language to a wistful, incomprehensible Romanian mumble suggested that she had. When she did not see what she sought, the disappointment soured her soul. Clouds rolled over the stars. She waited a long, long time, perhaps even falling asleep against the windowsill, although she did not think so. Annie did remember, though, that not witnessing God's benign face, she had wanted to, but could not, cry herself to sleep.

Often the occasion for another pogrom against the Jews in medieval and modern Europe, Easter in the Orthodox Church calendar is the holiest time of the year. Like Christmas, it also has elements especially appealing to a child's fancy, the most obvious being the ritual dyeing and presentation of coloured eggs. Romanian folk artists painted eggs as well as any Eastern European, detailing brilliant and minute geometric patterns, stylized flora, crosses and stars all over the fragile shells, after blowing out the yoke and white through pinholes pierced at either end. These decorated eggs satisfied aesthetic and symbolic purposes. Other eggs, dyed a solid red and blue and equally symbolic, satisfied the appetite.

On the first day of Easter an egg is placed in a pot of water. Annie remembered doing so for the children, according to Sophie's instructions, the woman from whom she learned a great deal about household and culinary matters, which stood her in good stead in later years. Then she also added a silver coin and, if available, a leaf or two of fresh basil to the water. Why, she never knew, it was just something they had done. Fresh basil not being handy, she sprinkled dried parsley, which Sophie grew in her garden and stored in a jar in the cupboard. Clever, perhaps, but not wise, because tradition maintained that everyone in the family should wash their faces with this water, a kind of ritual cleansing of the sins. My mother remembered Sophie's scowl, although she avoided a beating that day, as she brushed and picked minuscule bits of dried parsley off the faces of the children.

For some unaccountable reason that Easter morning, knowing the appalling consequences if she were caught, Annie sneaked into her aunt and uncle's bedroom, a forbidden chamber that the children never entered without permission. The black pipe from the kitchen stove rose through a hole in the floor and exited out a hole in the roof, so Sophie's room was always warm in the winter. A carved and painted wooden triptych of saintly images hung above the headboard of the bed. Multicoloured blankets, woven in Romania and carried in trunks overseas, covered a bulging straw-filled mattress. On the dresser draped with one of Sophie's elaborate doilies, in a mother-of-pearl dish, lay her string of black polished stone prayer beads, a gift from her grandmother before Sophie departed Romania for worlds unknown. Sophie seldom attended church services without the prayer beads twisted among the fingers of one hand. Next to them a candle in a brass stick and an icon of Saint Elisabeth. Annie quickly snatched the beads and hurried downstairs to tend to the eggs.

The first hard-boiled eggs, traditionally given to the children, were always red, a symbol of defence against evil: that, combined with burning Good Friday candles, which chased the Devil out of his hiding places, provided protection. The next lot of eggs, dyed blue, symbolized the affection of a young woman and portended good luck in matrimony. Although a solemn and holy time of the year for the Orthodox, Easter season was attended at moments with good humour and perhaps, certainly true in my mother's case, unexpressed skepticism. Coloured eggs are all very well, but if they are not eaten, rot sets in. The symbol becomes stench. The wonderfully intricately patterned eggs, hollowed out and not boiled, were kept as treasures or given as gifts; the solid-coloured hard-boiled eggs became part of the traditional egg-cracking ceremony and were eaten.

On Easter Sunday, oftentimes earlier, depending on the number of eggs and parental flexibility in matters ceremonial, each child held an egg in his or her fist and offered to crack it against another. Either the shells of both cracked, or the shell of only one did. The uncracked egg promised good luck in the future. Perhaps more tuned to religion than to rage at Eastertime, Sophie did not object if Annie participated in the cracking of eggs. Still close to their ancient association with creation, fertility, new life and luck, eggs were also somehow specifically commemorative of the passion of Christ. The person who struck the egg had to say, "Christ is risen" (*Cristos a Înviat*), a reminder of the occasion, and the other person replied, "It is true, He has risen" (*Adevărat a Înviat*). Annie did not remember if her eggs cracked more often than anyone else's. She shrugged the whole ceremony off as child's play, although she boiled and dyed eggs well after her own children had grown up and out of Orthodox rituals, developing a decided taste for shells dyed deep purple and yellow. By then she required no fragile symbols to predict the future.

Annie recalled riding on Samson's shoulders as her father walked around the church, one hand carrying a candle, the other grasping her ankle lest she fall. She saw pinpricks of fire dance in the chilly night as if a host of fireflies had gathered around her head and bobbed in front of her eyes. Her hands were tangled in his hair and beard as she hung on. Her older brothers and sisters, each carrying a candle, shoved against each other in the procession, Tinca carrying a baby wrapped in shawls. Driven to the church in the back of a hay wagon, half falling asleep but forcing herself to stay awake, Annie was clearly remembering the traditional, and very beautiful, ceremony of midnight mass (*Slujbă de Învierea*), followed by the candlelit procession of the faithful around the *biserică*.

Indeed, what could have been more enchanting and beautiful for the young child than an early spring night on the prairies, the sky a bowlful of stars, the freshly painted white church of Dysart glowing in the moonlight, hundreds of candles flickering under the breath of the spring breeze? In an ancient ceremony, replete with Byzantine paraphernalia and significance, ablaze under the prairie night within a few miles of the Saulteaux and Cree reserves, a crowd of Romanians joyously replied to the priest who had opened the doors to the church to announce that Christ had risen, that yes, indeed, He had risen! Even my mother shouted from the vantage point of her father's shoulders that Jesus was alive and well in Saskatchewan that night.

A mournful period for the Orthodox Christian, grieving for the death of Christ before experiencing the jubilation of His Resurrection, Easter was mercifully free from her aunt's predations, a delightful time of food and lights, jokes and brightly coloured eggs, merrier than Christmas, which had caused more pain than pleasure, intensifying her feelings of rejection. No one was more openly devout than Aunt Sophie at Eastertime. For at least three days, sometimes the entire Easter week, Annie was spared the rod or whatever utensil served the purpose. Not once did she remember crying or being beaten or hauled to the cowshed or deprived of food during the death and Resurrection of Jesus. Perhaps God was merciful, after all, or, as Annie later came to believe, merely arbitrary and more often than not oblivious to suffering. After a period of fasting observed during the forty days of Lent, particularly severe in Orthodox monasteries on Athos but modified on the Canadian prairie, the feast of Easter was celebrated with roast lamb, cottage cheese pie (*pasca*) and sponge or pound cake (*cozonac*).

On Good Friday, under Sophie's unforgiving eyes, Annie had mixed the nuts and poppy seeds in the cake mixture, poured it into the round pan lined with brown greased paper to prevent sticking, scraped the sides of the bowl—heavy brown crockery, heavier with the *cozonac* ingredients. Sophie insisted she hurry, stupid girl, and slipped the cake pan into the wood-heated oven. The roast lamb Sophie tended to herself, as well as the *pasca*. Having swept and washed the floors, shaken out the bed linens and hung them on the line, dusted the corners and the curtains, Annie carefully unwrapped Sophie's best dishes protected by cloth and layered on the two shelves in the glass-door cupboard of the parlour, dishes brought from Romania, her aunt said, although my mother doubted that. Her stomach caving in from the fast, Annie was ready for the feast, the first full-course meal of the season. Even in Aunt Sophie's house, she was fed on high holy days. Not every day, for Sophie used food against my mother as often as she used her hand, belt, broom or mixing spoon. No one should ever go hungry, my mother often said, and it was a lesson learned in the very depths of her own body. *Where there's no bread, pound cake will do*, says the proverb, referring to the traditional Easter *cozonac*.

Fasting did not deprive the growing children of nutrition, for allowances were always made, but where her own children received a full serving of bean soup during the period of fast, my mother received half. The hungry always count, and Annie counted the number of slices of homemade bread her cousins consumed to her one. When Eva, Sophie's oldest daughter and often sympathetic toward Annie, offered to share her food on the days when Aunt Sophie chose to punish the child for one real or imagined infraction or another, Annie refused. "It would stick in my throat and choke me," she said, admitting to severe hunger, not always in the name of righteous fasting. She refused to accept a portion allotted to someone else, as though doing so would have confirmed Sophie's right to deprive, would have relegated Annie to a status lower than Sophie's daughter, however kind the intent. It was better to go hungry and wait for the great Easter feast, she believed. She waited, swearing at the time never to deprive her own children of food, never to have so little that anyone, anyone at all in her own house when the day came, would feel the body-bending pain of hunger.

Sophie crossed herself many times in the church during the Resurrection midnight mass and sang the *doinele*. With Annie's constant assistance, she had prepared sufficient quantities to feed the village of Dysart itself. No Romanian woman with any sense of dignity and pride wanted her table considered lacking on a feast day. There must be enough, and more, for invited guests and for whoever else should knock on her door. Happy on the day of Resurrection, Sophie allowed even Annie to sit at the great wooden table and eat to her heart's content. Church services finished, Sophie had no need of her beads, which she clearly had not noticed missing from the dish under the severe eyes of the icon. After the meal, Sophie and her uncle retired to the parlour on this special occasion with the children to crack more eggs, leaving Annie to clear the mess. She gathered small portions of the *cozonac*, handfuls of nuts and raisins and a triangle of cheddar cheese in a small tea towel.

Shouting that she had to go to the outhouse, Annie hurried across the farmyard to the tackle shed where her aunt seldom went, tackle and harnesses not being her business. The chickens clucked and scurried away from her racing legs. From a wooden box with brown leather hinges and a rusted iron latch her uncle kept in a corner under an old wooden oxen yoke he no longer used, she retrieved a biscuit tin, a shortbread biscuit tin from England. Annie remembered a portrait of Queen Alexandra on the lid. The yoke was heavy, Annie strong. Thus far, her uncle had not opened the box and discovered her cache of food. Purloined from the kitchen over the past year or two, the food provided sustenance during periods of emergency to prevent her from fainting from hunger. Replenishing her supply, today she was quite satisfied. The Easter meal had done its good work in her stomach. She closed the lid and replaced the yoke. Annie then ran to the toilets, across the yard from the house and behind the chicken coop, an inconvenient distance in winter, but out of sight of anyone, like Aunt Sophie, who had the habit of looking through the windows.

Hoisting her skirt and removing the beads, Annie dropped them into one of the two holes of the toilet bench. The children often sat there two at a time. Holding her nose against the stench, she heard the beads plop gently into the swill, sounding like a baby's burp. It didn't matter if Sophie discovered who had taken the beads, although she would never know their excremental fate. Sooner or later Annie would be punished for something that she hadn't done, so she was prepared for another beating. But not today! Easter, indeed, was a glorious time of the year. God was great!

Part Three

Uscatele (Rabbit Ears)

3 cups flour
6 eggs
½ teaspoon salt
icing sugar
2 cups vegetable oil for deep-frying

- *Sift flour and salt into a bowl.*
- *Add eggs and mix until dough is stiff.*
- *Roll dough until very thin, and cut into strips 2 by 5 inches.*
- *Cut a slit in the centre of each strip and pull one end of the strip through the slit.*
- *Deep-fry until light brown.*
- *Drain and dust with icing sugar.*

Makes approximately 3 dozen.

CHAPTER 13

The best food to eat is what I make myself.

When not in school, Annie was happiest with a hoe in hand. She quickly developed the skill necessary to plant and maintain a substantial vegetable garden. Occasionally her aunt also worked in the patch beside her, after Uncle had dumped the manure, which Sophie and Annie then spread and dug into the soil with pitchfork and spade. Behind the barn, a heap of animal manure steamed in the sun and dried, breaking down into rich fertilizer over the year. Always dig from the bottom after shovelling aside the first layer. That's where the richness lies. Freshly plopped manure burns the roots of young plants.

Annie acquired a personal relationship with this garden, which in her imagination she regarded as her own, and during February and March dreamed of planting time in the spring. All her life she held a kind of wistful attitude toward gardening, her mind so preoccupied when she was bent over tomato and sweet-pepper plants that she wouldn't hear anyone call her from the porch. The vigour and abundance of her houseplants led people to say she possessed a proverbial "green thumb," ascribing magical influence to skill and knowledge that they lacked. Nothing grew from magic. Annie worked the land too long to believe in that superstition. When she had a yard as an adult, however small the plot, she managed a garden; when she did not, the dream of the garden nourished and sustained.

In the middle of the beans or cabbages, Sophie never struck Annie, so my mother came to see the garden as a place of refuge, the physical presence of her aunt inspiring neither anxiety nor fear as long as Annie stayed on the few hundred square metres of her magical terrain.

Once the soil was prepared and turned over, it was dangerous to plant too early, depending on the vegetable. Onions, beets and peas can be sowed as soon as the soil is workable, resistant to spring frost; other seeds like squashes will rot in cold earth or simply not germinate. Tomato seedlings, like the ones sown and coddled in the house by Aunt Sophie several weeks before planting time, must wait until the risk of frost has passed, which, on the prairies, is anyone's guess. By the seventh Sunday after Easter, *Duminică Mare*, Great Sunday or the day of Pentecost, Annie had sown the cold-resistant seeds. The church floor had been strewn with grass and early spring flowers, a practice repeated in Romanian homes. Particular about the cleanliness of her floors, Sophie had never been keen about littering them with flora, knowing full well the difficulty of removing grass stains from the braided rugs. Instead, over the doorway she hung a clutch of grass tied in the middle with a string. A celebration symbolizing expectation of good crops, the seventh Sunday after Easter provided the occasion for feasting. The third or fourth week of May was also a good time to think about placing the tomato plants, although my mother always waited until the beginning of June.

After the religious festivities of the Easter season, Sophie also welcomed spring. Never afraid of getting her hands dirty, Annie loved to delve into the soil, to understand its requirement by feel, a process she carried over into cooking. Touch was as important as taste.

Taught by Sophie, she didn't learn about gardening from books, but from experience. If the onions are planted too closely together, they require more water, and if the onion bed is not weeded regularly, the bulbs do not expand to good-sized globes because they expend energy competing with weeds. Watch out for bolting, a problem also with lettuces. Water tenuous beet seedlings carefully along the edges of the row to avoid washing them out of the soil. Radish seeds mixed with the carrots help to identify the location and to loosen the soil. It's impossible to shovel too much well-aged shit under a tomato plant.

Cabbages are heavy feeders, requiring an even supply of moisture to prevent the heads from cracking and sufficient compost to nourish the roots. To retard the maturing process if you are not ready to harvest, carefully fork around one side of the plant and raise just enough to loosen the roots. Cabbages taste better, like rutabaga, after a frost, sweetened by the cold. Beets, less demanding, can look after themselves more or less, if properly thinned and weeded. Tomatoes, riskier but not impossible to cultivate to their full and juicy ripeness on the prairies, given the likelihood of early frosts, also flourish where their thirst is quenched and the soil has been heavily manured. Onions benefit from the addition of wood ash to the soil; their sweetness is determined by moisture, and dry soil will intensify the sharp flavour and the sulphur compounds that cause the eyes to water. The ash also helps deter the onion maggot. At least the repellent tomato hornworm can be picked off by hand, if you are not squeamish. It's a good idea to grow dill because the creature seems equally attracted to the herb. If Annie saw a hornworm, she pinched it off with her bare fingers and threw it at the younger children, who often played at the edge of the garden while she worked. Squashes also demand a consistent supply of food and drink if they are to mature on the vine before the cold sets in. A touch of frost causes squash leaves to repine.

Annie loved the look of first frost in the fall, especially the sugary coating it gave to late-blooming chrysanthemums, but she knew its devastating effect on sensitive vegetables. I remember helping my mother cover tomato plants with sheets as protection against a damaging frost. She told me how she and her older cousins used to run to the garden at sunset, often as early as the third week of August, flapping Aunt Sophie's sheets because the temperature was going to drop to zero or a degree or two lower. Carrots and turnips benefit from a nip of frost, which sweetens their flavour. Tomatoes and peppers don't. Each child gripping a corner, Annie and her cousins opened the sheets, laughing as the cloth billowed above their heads before deflating and sinking to rest lightly on the tops of the pepper plants. They secured the edges against the wind with rocks. Under the moonlight, the sheeted vegetables looked like rows of freshly fallen snow.

In the morning, after dawn and the rising of the temperature, they removed the sheets, somewhat heavy with frosty dew, the plants beneath saved. Aunt Sophie designated certain sheets, usually the oldest and most worn, for this task and none other. Occasionally, depending on the size of the garden and the number of rows to be protected, more sheets were required. If once or twice Sophie's very best sheets, the ones she had embroidered with birds and flowers for exclusive use on her own bed, found their way in the garden under frosty moonlight, Annie enjoyed risking her aunt's wrath. Torn between relief that her vegetables had been saved and rage over the violation of her linen, Aunt Sophie threatened dire punishment, but even she recognized that the children had little choice in the matter. Acting on her express commands to protect the plants, they used everything they could find. How could she blame them?

Working in the vegetable garden one early June Saturday, when Sophie's children had been assigned to other duties on the farm and Sophie herself had gone to the town of Lipton with her husband to buy supplies, Annie noticed a group of darkly clothed people walking up the gentle slope of the road leading to the house. Under the soaring and singing spring sky of Saskatchewan, everyone was visible for quite a distance. Behind them Annie could make out the wheels of a wagon, huge, heavily spoked wheels as high as she was tall. Some furniture seemed to be piled in the back. She wondered why they hadn't driven the wagon up the road to the farmhouse. Almost blue in the distance, the horse stood motionless on the grid road. As the group approached, she was still unable to make out who they were. Although people would not think twice about walking a few miles or so to visit someone on a fine day, time permitting, during spring there was precious little opportunity for casual visiting. All her school friends had their own chores to complete before being allowed to play or go for spectacularly long walks on the prairie, delve into the coulees or explore the sloughs. As a rule Sophie disapproved of unexpected visitors unless they were family. Annie raised her hand to shield her eyes from the sun.

The breeze played around Annie's faded print dress, a hand-me-down, not from Sophie who passed her clothes on to her own daughters, but from a neighbouring farm woman whose daughter had died a year ago. The dress didn't fit properly; either because it had shrunk or because my mother had grown, she didn't remember which. Annie was always shrugging to adjust the seams around the shoulders, which cut into her flesh. Most of the clothes my mother wore as a child in Aunt Sophie's house did not fit her. She hoisted the skirts or pulled at the blouses or tugged at the necklines, felt the cloth stretch too tightly over her back when she bent. God forbid she should ever rip a dress—Aunt Sophie would see that she paid hell for it. The other children ran about easily in clothes that fit, but Annie occasionally tried to stretch the length of

her skirt by grasping the hem and pushing down hard. She succeeded only in making the length uneven. When the clothes were
wet and she hung them on the line in warm weather, she tried to
stretch the fabric to make it wider or longer.

One day that past winter, when the dresses and dungarees
hung so stiff on the line that they creaked and cracked in the wind
like decapitated bodies strung up against the diamond frigidity
of the January sky, Annie took a horsewhip from her uncle's
tackle shed and whipped two of her hand-me-down dresses. One
had a print of ribboned bouquets of Indian blanket flowers,
which grew wild by the thousands in parts of the land that had
not been cultivated. Unconcerned whether Sophie spied her
through the window, Annie removed her muffler to breathe
more easily and loosened the buttons of her heavy wool coat.
Then she slashed at the stiff dresses the way her aunt slashed at
her back with her uncle's belt. She whipped until her arms were
weary from the exertion. As the fabric softened and thawed from
the heat of flagellation, it became pliable and began wrapping
itself around the whip.

She stopped, her lungs chilled from breathing in winter air
through her mouth. The clothes hung limp and damply warm to
the touch of her cheek. When she tried them on later, they still
did not fit properly. She had even imagined rolling them up and
burning them in the Quebec heater in the parlour in which fires
were built only on the coldest days. And Aunt Sophie seemed to
have a great tolerance for cold rooms. Annie could see her breath
in the parlour on New Year's Day. Wood wasn't so readily available that they could burn it every day for non-cooking purposes.
Nor did coal drop from the sky.

None of my mother's efforts to adjust the clothes to fit her
angular body to a degree of comfort succeeded. Whatever she
wore, her body resisted. Irritated beyond patience, she fidgeted in

ill-fitting clothes until the teacher ordered her to sit still or spend the rest of the morning standing in the corner. Her feet callused, or her toes scrunched and hurting from improperly fitting shoes, or boots so large on her tortured feet that they made a smacking sound when she walked until she stuffed them with newspaper, Annie yearned for the day when she'd be able to go to Regina. A fabulous city of stores and movie houses, electric lights and phonographs—she knew because her own teacher had visited the city more than once and told the class stories about crowds of people bustling along paved streets, hotels that glittered in the night and automobile accidents! Her sister Tenka, whom Annie hadn't seen for several years, now lived there. Where Tenka lived, Annie knew in her heart that she would live, too. Annie promised herself that one day she'd go right into the biggest Regina store and choose a dress off the rack, a dress that clothed her like a cloud. It didn't have to be silk or satin, but the seams wouldn't dig into her armpits and the waist wouldn't be too high or too low, so she could walk as elegantly and comfortably as the Queen of Romania.

While hoeing between the rows in the garden, she would have preferred to wear a pair of her cousin's work dungarees, her own pair waiting to be washed after she had mucked in the pigsty yesterday. The boots too large for her feet, she stuffed them with the Cupar newspaper. They slapped against her calves.

The strangers wore very long, dark coats and skirts. From Annie's perspective above them in the garden, the coats and dresses appeared to brush against the muddy soil. Spring run-off and rains had softened the earth. For days, the ground squished and sighed when she walked upon it in bare feet, although the elevated garden bed had drained sufficiently to allow work to proceed. The roads were rutted and ridged with coils of now drying mud that looked like the rolls of hair some of the women wore under their nets and kerchiefs on Sunday.

As the strangers approached, Annie could see that the group consisted of a man, two women and one child, a girl of about her age. One of the women had a checkered shawl draped over her back, fringed, trailing almost to the ground. The other woman wore a black kerchief like a widow still in mourning over the death of her husband. The dresses of both ladies, as they walked up the incline toward Annie, were patterned and voluminous, like the dresses Annie had seen in the school books, worn by women before the Great War. Some of the old Romanian women still wore dresses like that. You could never see their legs. The man, with a flowered woman's kerchief tied around his neck, carried a wide-brimmed hat and wore a green vest under a brown suit coat. His hair was very black and fell over his ears to his shoulders.

The long hair immediately identified him as one of the Native people, whom Annie called Indians, who lived on reserves not far away. The girl's head was covered with a boy's cap, and she wore boy's clothes. Unsmiling, they approached with their shoulders rounded and heads slightly bowed as if acknowledging the presence of royalty under the prairie sky. Each member of the party carried a bag or a large pouch, all stuffed full. From the edge of the garden, overlooking the rows of seedlings, the older of the two women, her brown, weather-beaten face heavily creased, began speaking in a language Annie did not understand. The man seemed to nod in agreement and smiled with a closed mouth. The girl clung to the younger woman's hand and hid behind the blue cornflowered skirt of her dress.

Annie understood little about Indians, nothing about their situation in Saskatchewan at this time, although many Romanians bought firewood from the Gordon Reserve in the Touchwood Hills, a more heavily treed area than the wheat fields. The Native peoples had also assisted Jewish immigrants in the Lipton area when times were difficult and food scarce. Her father's farm was not far from the hills through which flowed the Jumping Deer River. The Crees and Saulteaux had agreed to share southern Saskatchewan, when it was called the Northwest Territories, with the immigrants in exchange for reserve land, annuities and tax exemptions. Although she had learned a few things about Indians in her school, perhaps a passing reference to the 1876 Treaty Four by which the Crees and Saulteaux granted the use of the land for the economic, political, social and spiritual purposes of the newcomers, Romanians among them, Annie knew nothing about their real lives on the reserve, nothing about what they believed, what they felt, how they actually lived. Hence, one of the peculiarities of history: a Byzantine Orthodox church erected by immigrants, dispossessed in Romania, laying claim to land under the auspices of the Canadian government, in territory over which thousands of buffalo once roamed and Native peoples enjoyed unrestricted rights of hunting and movement. A young girl whose mind and heart were still so closely tied to her father's memory and culture, Annie instinctively crossed herself, as if warding off the presence of the evil eye, feeling some trepidation in the middle of her vegetable garden until the Indians began speaking.

She still imagined circles of teepees, smoke puffing out of the top, and travois on which the people pulled all their worldly possessions behind their horses. She had seen pictures. The clothes also surprised her. No intricate designed beadwork, no fringed deerskin jackets, no feathers crowning their heads. Just dark clothes very much like the ones any poor Romanian in Canada would have worn that day. The man switched from his language to a flat-toned English, lacking the rhythms of Romanian, scarcely audible, his words whirling and curling like feathers blown back by the wind. The women's dresses billowed and rippled, the fabric rustling like the buzz of bees swirling inebriated over a pail of rotten apples. My mother wondered if the cloth had been starched; she couldn't account for the sound of it, although she still remembered the brush and buzz for decades. Although they were strangers, their manner assuaged Annie's anxieties. She had no reason to fear them; they had only made her nervous. That was the very first time she had actually met an Indian, but she had sometimes seen them walking in groups of three or four on the dusty main road of Dysart in the summer, parcels under their arms.

They did not move in any threatening way, not like Aunt Sophie; they were not armed. She knew that the Plains Indians had once hunted with bows, shooting arrows at stampeding buffalo from their horses. Her books said so. The man's smile broadened, and Annie could see that he had few if any teeth. The old woman kept nodding and started speaking in her native dialect, to whom Annie did not know, for she directed her words at no one in particular, kept scanning the sky above my mother's head, sometimes pointing to the garden, sometimes to the wagon down on the grid road.

The man asked if he could help her, if there was any work. They would do much for very little, for a few coins, if she had any to spare, or some food. They were looking for work, having travelled many miles, trundling in their wagon from one village to another, from one farm to another, camping near the sloughs if the farmers permitted, sometimes devising shelter in the coulees. The younger woman kept her eyes to the ground. Well, what could Annie do? She had no authority to hire anyone to work on her uncle's farm, and she certainly had no money to give away. The vegetables were too young to serve any purpose, certainly not ready to satisfy hunger. Come with me, she said, dropping the hoe, her boots slapping against her calves, and ran toward the kitchen door.

She told the man to give her his hat, and the man, seeming to understand her purpose, did not hesitate. The bread had been baked that morning, three loaves, heavy and nutritious with unbleached whole wheat grains, and in the pantry were jars of pickled beets and cucumbers, which she herself had canned last September, smoked bacon seasoned with paprika, her uncle's favourite, a basket of eggs, some of which had been gathered that very morning, thick and pink homemade sausages bolstered with globules of fat and redolent with spice, sacks of sugar and flour and tins of precious raisins and poppy seeds and a tray of cold cheese *plăcintă*, a wedge of cheddar cheese under a bowl, and more food than Auntie's family could consume in a week— surely enough to spare, surely Sophie and Tudor wouldn't notice, and if they did, why would they mind? Why would anyone mind feeding a hungry person? She placed four eggs in the hat, two pieces of sausage—and here my mother held her hands apart to indicate the length—half a loaf of bread, for she could say the children ate the other half, and she didn't know if she gave them cheese or *plăcintă*. She dipped into the tin of raisins and dropped a fistful into the man's hat.

Outside she returned the hat, heavy now with stolen food. He said he would clean the chicken house, could not take the food without giving something back in return. Worried that her aunt and uncle would return, Annie told him that now wasn't the time. But if he returned in the fall, August even, her uncle needed extra help with the crops, then he could find work. Hesitant, perhaps hunger overcoming reluctance and pride, he accepted the hat filled with food and nodded. The old woman broke into a chant. The younger woman smiled, her eyes so dark that they looked like Sophie's prayer beads. The Natives turned and walked down the slope, the dresses swishing and buzzing with starch, the little girl, fist in mouth, staring back at Annie who remained by the kitchen door. Hurry, she wanted to shout, don't let my aunt see you.

From that time on, Annie became more aware of the Native people, not as silent, shadowy figures appearing on the periphery, but dark-eyed—eyes browner than cattails—people who, she knew, lived on reserves, often indigent and wandering, looking for work. Her aunt spoke disparagingly of Indians, despising them the way she despised Romanian Gypsies, saying one was no better than the other. Sophie confused nomadic behaviour with shiftlessness and thievery, not for a moment understanding the sad irony of historical events that allowed her husband to plough the land and her niece to dig a garden in Indian territory. My mother lacked historical perspective as well. She did not, however, deny food when she had it to give, even to a Gypsy if he knocked on her door.

CHAPTER 14

The Devil can hide in a pile of stones.

Above the head is heaven, beneath the feet hell. The earth between is not always the pathway to God or a refuge from Satan. Despite the mythology of idylls and pastorals, agricultural life in the first decades of the past century was anything but the Eden of poetic imagination. Although the propaganda posters of the Canadian government promised paradise to lure European peasantry to the Indian lands of the Canadian prairies, the farm remained one of the most dangerous places on earth for the unskilled and unwary to raise children. The farm at its worst broke backs, cracked bones, severed hands, mangled feet, coarsened skin, stunted intellect, limited horizons and wearied spirits. A long tradition of contempt for farmers and labourers who work with their hands survives to this day in cultural attitudes.

What Annie knew of paradise and poetry, she learned in the schoolhouse; what she knew of the Devil, she learned on Sophie's farm. If her imagination attempted to soar like the mythical bird of Romania, the demands of work and the pain of punishment dragged it back down to the furrows of the fields. She was never afraid of work, and her hands toughened and blistered. Nor did she complain, but the daily tension between the practical and fanciful dissipated concentration. With a desire to imagine the future, she often forgot the present. This attribute is necessary for scientists and artists, but unfortunate for a working girl boiling diapers or bathing babies or canning fruit or baking bread or ploughing the field. Inattention leads to disaster. The accident, almost always avoidable, occurs when the mind flies through the Saskatchewan sky rather than focusing on the land.

Of all the incidents in her childhood, Annie regarded the terrible accident with the horse and plough as the worst and wove Sophie's malice into her narration of the event as if her aunt somehow had managed to produce the harmful result. My mother remained enough of a peasant woman in her old age to look for essentially fantastic explanations and demonic influences in life, much the way people choose to believe that alien beings, callously indifferent to the hard work of the farmer and the potential economic loss, carve out crop circles in their grain fields. Annie had only personal experience and her Transylvanian heritage to provide all the evidence she needed: it was indeed good to light a candle to the Devil every now and then. Magic and superstition rushed in where reason failed.

It was not unusual for Saskatchewan children to be harnessed to a plough. When they had reached suitable age and strength, they were put to work. Child labour laws, if any, did not really apply. So many different kinds of ploughs: the sulky plough, designed to break the soil and requiring several horses; the gang plough, also requiring six horses and used for summer fallowing; and the iron hand-held plough, harnessed to one or two horses. Samson had owned oxen to work his land. No mean possessions.

Sophie and her husband, Tudor, had prospered, had extended their agricultural domain beyond the initial quarter section, had hired help by the mid-twenties. Annie was correct in assuming her uncle would be interested in the Native workers if they cared to return. Uncle Tudor's prejudice gave way to cheap labour. Although her aunt and uncle depended more and more on mechanized farm machinery, they still needed their children, as they matured, to help out on the land. The weather could change suddenly, and the more hands, the more machinery and tools employed, the faster the work got done before a week-long deluge ruined ploughing prospects. Everyone worked. Annie was not being malevolently exploited, although she tended to forget that the other children also trudged behind the plough, guiding the blade, as the horses or oxen dragged it through the soil.

The plough (*plug*), real and symbolic, featured greatly in the lives of Romanian peasants, not surprising for an agricultural people. It's a measure of how close the ties that bound my mother and her family to old Romania that Annie remembered the rituals involving the plough. As she felt her boots slap against the back of her calves, one foot ahead of the other between the raised sides of the furrow dredged up by the plough, she held the ends of each wooden handle rising diagonally from the iron blade. The hooves of one horse were attached to the plough by ropes. With its back feet always ahead of the blade and its coarse tail swishing flies off its hind legs, the horse plopped and trudged in the still-damp earth. Annie found it easy to let her eyes search the sky, to let her mind fill in the enormity of the blue with characters and images from the stories she'd heard in school. If she listened very carefully, she could hear the train on the other side of the farm trundling toward Dysart, the train she promised herself that she would take one day. Her brother John, unhappy in school, unhappy in his foster home, swore he would run alongside it one day, hop into one of the open boxcars and disappear for good. No one was going to keep him down on the farm. This pale boy, who kept his eyes down and sporadically attended school—the only place she could see him, for he almost never appeared in church—would soon disappear from her life like her sisters and her oldest brother, Nick.

Every year before Christmas, some of the farmers scraped the mud off a hand plough, washed and polished the blade and placed the plough on display in the church hall. Women and children decorated the handles with red and blue ribbons and paper streamers. It looked like a plough out of a fairy tale, the kind only mythical horses with silver manes and golden hooves dragged over the land.

Annie loved colours. When Sophie ripped a red ribbon out of the girl's black hair, Annie tied it more tightly around her braid. When Sophie tugged the braid until she yanked the hair out of Annie's skull to the point of scalping, Annie bit her tongue from the pain, held her hands against the sides of her head and screamed. The next time, she shoved the red ribbon in her underpants and walked to school on more than one occasion feeling the ribbon against her skin. Before classes began, she went to the girl's outhouse and retrieved the ribbon to tie it into a bow like a red floppy flower on her black hair.

The feast and celebration of *Plugusorul* meant more than a pretty plough. To Annie's amazement, a man stood above the handles and recited a poem without a moment's hesitation. For Annie, who still covered her mouth to hide her crooked teeth when she laughed, who shifted and twisted and scratched beneath ill-fitting clothes, standing up and speaking in front of a crowd of people, family or not, filled her with terror. Standing and speaking in the classroom without collapsing or running out of the school required enormous willpower. The exercise strained her nerves. Often her voice went flat, dying in an incoherent whisper on a dry thick tongue. Speak louder, Annie! We can't hear you! Rather than drawing attention to herself, she always found it better to remain quiet and secretive. But even a quiet mouse could be snatched up by a hawk and torn to pieces by a sharp, curved beak. A chicken sitting quietly on its nest of eggs could be grabbed and carried to the block, all its clucking and squawking ineffective against the swift, assured chop of the axe.

The day was warm, the breeze light, the sweat dampening the red ribbon in her underpants. The field stretched beyond her seeing until it met the sky, the land rising, the sky lowering, kissing each other on the horizon. She had begun the ploughing just after a breakfast of *colivă*, bread and tea. Even Sophie thought it wise that her niece be well fed for the work in the fields. She packed Annie a lunch of cheese, bread and pieces of paprika-sprinkled pork fat and gave her a Mason jar of water. And, shaking a pudgy finger in front of the girl's face, she admonished Annie not to return home until she had ploughed an acre, if she knew what was good for her. The ploughing did not sound like an onerous task to Annie; she had turned the soil before, and she liked the horse, the fly-swishing motion of its tail, the evenness of its trudge through the soil as if the animal were keeping time to music, and she would be alone, out of Sophie's reach.

During the *Plugusorul* festivities, the man who recited the poem in the church hall appealed to God to help the farmers, to keep the crops of the new year from drought, deluge, grasshoppers and disease, from whatever the Devil fancied would spoil the efforts of the faithful. And as he chanted the words in a nasal whine, several boys ran yelling and laughing around the little raised platform at one end of the hall, slashing whips in the air and over the backside of whatever make-believe animal was harnessed to the gorgeous multi-ribboned plough. The boys on stage, some of them her classmates, also rang bells similar to the one the teacher rang in the schoolyard, the kind hung from cattle, big, clanking, ear-splitting bells that caused all the Romanians in the hall to break into laughter and applaud. Sophie and her children also laughed, Sophie removing a white handkerchief from her hefty bosom to wipe away the tears of joy in her eyes. Sophie seldom laughed at home.

Annie loved the celebration, especially the meal in the church hall, where not even Sophie stopped her from enjoying her favourite dish, *pui cu smântână*, cream of chicken stew. The chicken was soft and delicate to taste, the cream thinned with chicken fat and laden with spice; she couldn't get enough of it, and because the entire family was in a public place and Romanians cooked enough to feed the world, there was always more for second and third helpings. She only wished she could have somehow hidden and carried a portion home to eat the next day. But she didn't want to mix it with her raisins and *mititei* (cured sausages) in Queen Alexandra's tin.

So, if the *Plugusorul* prayers were answered, then ploughing the field on a spring day was the least of Annie's worries. And the land was not especially stony, although eons of stone slowly rose to the surface, pushed up by frost, and primordial bits of rock gathered in the rolls of the earth. Uncle and the boys usually picked up the larger stones and either piled them in the middle of the field or carted and dumped them behind one of the sheds, for even rocks could be useful for walls and foundations. Still, this was not rocky terrain and stones did not prevent ploughing.

Annie was not troubled by the thought of rocks. It was enough that Sophie stayed in the house that day. God had answered her prayers as well, even though her scalp hurt still when she brushed her hair. One day, she would walk over her own land, and she would plant not just cabbages and beets and horseradish but roses, redder than blood, and marigolds as orange as the setting sun. She had seen roses in a few yards in Dysart, had even leaned over a fence and, careful not to prick her hands, fondled the petals of one until the front door opened and an English voice yelled at her to get away from the roses. Not at all like the old German or Hungarian woman in black on another street who had kindly invited her into the yard. A red rose bush against the blue prairie sky, the scent of its soft, many-layered flowers carried by the breeze. She would ask Johnny to live with her, and somehow her sisters and Nick would also return, and they'd create acres and acres of roses, red as her heart's desire, to cover the recently ploughed fields.

Attached to the hand plough, the horse stood waiting in the field for instructions. It was a horse Annie had never seen before, borrowed for the occasion from a neighbouring farmer. Uncle's own horse suffered in the stall from constricted bowels. People helped each other during ploughing, planting and harvesting seasons. A neighbour who spurned his neighbours did not survive on his own efforts. So Annie began, initially staring down at the blade, recently sharpened, but not for long. Her mind preoccupied with stories and visions of the future, she and the horse stepped out of rhythm, and it began to drag faster than she could walk. Farm horses are not racers or jumpers, but they can bolt if not properly trained. Annie had let her familiarity with her uncle's horse cloud her perception of this new animal, and she was feeling unsteady behind the plough.

Then it happened. She never really knew why, but she attributed the cause of the incident to a sudden flock of squalling crows that rose up from the fields in front and startled the horse. The mare's front legs kicked up and she broke first into a trot, then, warming to the exercise, she hurtled forward and began running as fast as the weight of the plough would allow. Instead of letting go, terrified of what would happen if the horse ran away and she had to explain herself to Sophie, Annie hung on and began running too, shouting *Whoa!* and trying to keep up with the horse and plough. Her boots slipped on the earth over the churned-up lumps of soil. She called to the horse to stop, but unaccustomed to a weak voice from a stranger, unrestrained and panicked, the horse galloped, and then the pointed plough's blade hit a rock just beneath the surface of the soil.

The blade tipped and the handles lifted high off the ground, Annie still hanging on. Half-running and half-jumping, she felt herself suddenly hoisted and thrown. She somersaulted in the air over the handles behind the horse's ass, the sky appearing between her booted feet, dirt flying like a flurry of black snow. For a moment she was a huge, wingless and clumsy bird circling in the air above the blade before she plummeted. The horse stopped as suddenly as it had bolted, and Annie's head, narrowly missing the blade, struck the earth first. Several stones slapped against her cheeks in midair, and one piece of ancient rock smacked against her right eye when she hit ground. Beneath the swish of the horse's tail, she lay between rows of churned-up earth, her arm bent and twisted behind her back, although the bones had not been broken.

A wet stream dribbled out of her injured eye. Annie touched her cheek and saw her fingers covered with blood, red as the rose, red as the ribbon in her hair. She lay under the blue prairie sky, dirt in her mouth, the horse's tail fanning her face, wondering if she was dying. She lay there for a long time, until flies settled on her nose. The sky had turned the colour of sunset, and, disoriented and winded, Annie imagined for a moment that the sky had opened after all. The blue doors of the heavens had parted and God would reveal himself. She heard crows in the distance and the snorting of the horse, impatiently waiting for instructions. She managed to pull herself up to her knees, so shaken and sore that she doubted she could stand. How could she finish the ploughing, her eye bleeding, her muscles throbbing, her legs wobbly? What if the horse bolted again?

In the distance she heard shouting, and through her bloody eye saw Aunt Sophie, skirts raised above her bulgy knees, trundling across the field like a cow in boots, with several of Annie's cousins racing ahead, and one or two other people she didn't recognize. Her head tilted to one side as if weighted with lead, and the pain streaking behind her eyeball, originating somewhere in the core of her brain, made her ears ring. She was dizzy and grasped a handle of the plough, only to feel the horse begin to walk forward. For some reason Annie allowed herself to be dragged a few feet along the furrow, dirt and pebbles kicking into her open mouth. It was hard to breathe.

Harder when Sophie grabbed her by the hair and slapped her face, causing the injured eye to roll in its socket. My mother cried out and saw Sophie's hand about to strike again, held back above her shoulder because she noticed the bleeding eye. *Prost, prost, cioară!* She helped Annie stand, wiping her face with the hand-kerchief pulled out of her bodice. Once in the house, weak from shock and pain, my mother said all she wanted to do was go to bed, not even wash her face, but Sophie forced her head under the pump, and cold water splashed all over Annie's head as her aunt rubbed. She did not send one of the children to find Uncle and tell him to hurry back to the house and drive Annie to the doctor's office in Cupar. She scrubbed the dirt out of Annie's hair, off her neck, off her face, the water mingling with the blood, then wrapped a clean tea towel over Annie's head, bandaging the injured eye. The eyeball had not been gouged out, the child had not been blinded, for she said she could see, and no bones were broken. A cut, a bruise, a drop of blood. Sophie had nursed many a sick and injured child. Doctors cost money. Where was the time? The fields needed to be ploughed.

What a doctor could have done in those days for Annie is a matter of conjecture. There was nerve damage, a blood clot, Annie discovered years later, and the eye never fully recovered its perfect vision or its natural position. Bad enough she had crooked teeth, and now a crooked eye! It was the slap, my mother said, the slap across her bloodied face in the very middle of her agony, the refrain of *prost, prost, prost*, the harsh and relentless lack of sympathy or concern, that permanently solidified Sophie into the monster of my mother's memory. She did not have to finish the ploughing, at least—even Sophie saw how ineffectually Annie would have performed the task under the circumstances. She was allowed to sit by the kitchen table while Sophie gutted and washed the chickens for the stew. One can behead chickens on the tree stump or, simply and more efficiently, one can grab and snap their necks with a flick of the wrist. Sophie was a fast and proficient killer. Hens, snatched off the face of the earth by their horny feet, did not stand a chance. Into a cauldron of boiling water Sophie had plunked the birds. Hot water allows for easier plucking of the feathers.

While Annie sobbed quietly so as not to annoy her aunt, Eva offered to make Annie a cup of tea. For once Sophie did not object, although she said it was a waste. Annie didn't need tea, Sophie said, she needed to pay attention. She had a good mind to take the belt to her. Let that be a lesson, Sophie told the girls, as if the sole purpose of Annie's existence was to warn Sophie's own children how not to behave. A simple task, a simple chore to hold the handle of the plough. What child your age couldn't do such a thing and do it well? Annie heard the words but found it hard to keep awake; something in her head kept pulling her down into a stupor. You'll survive—just a little scratch. Pay attention. Learn something. As Sophie hacked through skin and bone to separate a chicken's leg from its body, Annie dozed off.

CHAPTER 15

The old hen makes the best soup.

Such vegetables as endured the long, hard months of winter storage now found themselves, after being washed, peeled, quartered, sliced or chopped, boiling down to a limp grey in the stewpot. The rutabaga, carrots and potatoes, leached of their colour and nutrition, clouded the broth. Annie added salt, dill, parsley and pepper to taste. Fennel was more desirable, but dill served. In the afternoon, Uncle Tudor had returned home from his supply trip to Lipton with mushrooms, a miracle this time of the year, so Aunt declared that she would make *ciorbă* for supper. The juice from the sauerkraut crock would sour the soup base. Annie was instructed to stir the pot, heat the mushrooms sprinkled with spices in an iron skillet until browned. The kitchen was not a large room, no more than ten by ten, crowded by a great wooden table and several chairs in the middle, the McClary range on one wall, the black stovepipe leading to the second floor, the icebox, the sideboard, the dish cupboard, crocks along another and a sink standing on its own legs under the window with a pump. By now, Annie had memorized every pot and pan, dish and cup, spoon and knife, where everything was stored and shelved, as adroit in her aunt's kitchen as she would eventually become in her own, happiest in the midst of food.

The farm lane to the grid road had been cleared of snow. Take the horse and wagon, Aunt Sophie had encouraged her husband over the breakfast bowls of *colivă*, distrusting the wheels of the car, but Uncle said the snow had been flattened and hardened over the past two or three days by local traffic and he could drive. It would have taken much too long to travel by horse for the supplies that the Dysart store seemed unable to stock. The sky was clear, with no threat of another storm like the one that had dumped so much snow on top of what had already fallen in February. God willing, they'd seen the last blizzard of the season before the spring thaw. The mushrooms in a brown waxed-paper-lined box, which Uncle handed to Sophie like a newborn baby, elicited ravenous gasps among the children, who rarely saw so many white-capped mushrooms in such quantity. A treasure for *ciorbă*, the sour soup everyone loved so much, the mushrooms had to be used that very day.

All the other children, except for the babies, had wrapped themselves in their various coats and scarves, mittens and boots, hats and caps and left for school. Annie was too old to cry anymore; tears accomplished nothing except to arouse Sophie's wrath. The day before, her aunt had insisted that Annie no longer needed to attend school. Sophie sent a note with Eva to give to the teacher. Annie, now fourteen, would no longer be a pupil in her class. What happened to Annie then had happened and would happen to many other children, their forced withdrawal from formal education constituting an intellectual waste of tragic proportions.

Schooling had been a refuge from brutality and a release from childhood despair, an introduction to possibilities Annie could scarcely imagine on the farm itself. Superior in achievement to any of her cousins, her English improving, Annie had begun to read the books on her own, to commit some of the stories to memory, and had allowed herself, for one brief, illusory moment, to believe that high school in Fort Qu'Appelle or even Regina lay within her grasp. When Sophie, armed with a rolling pin, had broken the terrible news, Annie could have run screaming out of the house, even barefoot, something she had done often enough before. But she knew it would be a waste of time. She felt as if she were dying on the spot, even though her heart beat loudly enough for her to hear. She didn't scream, she didn't cry, she didn't argue. The bitter disappointment hit so hard, so suddenly, shattering her dreams, that a kind of chill entered her soul and numbed her sensibilities. She stood shivering in the unheated parlour where Sophie told her in front of the table of icons, their flaking gold halos dimmed by a thin layer of frost.

In recognition of the many Romanian students in her class, the teacher had planned special activities for the first of March, *martisor*. Annie, as one of the oldest, had been asked to help the younger boys and girls cut out red and white decorations to pin or tape around the room. There would be stories, red and white ribbons, and little gifts, a candy or a coin, but still, a gift was not to be despised. On *martisor*, Romanians wished their friends and family good health, good fortune and everlasting happiness. And if you had a special friend, he would also give you something. Annie enjoyed no such friendship, but other girls did and she was happy for them. She still possessed her special red ribbon, washed for the occasion, which she had planned to wear around her wrist, a symbol of blood. Some of the children would wear white threads pinned on their clothes, a sign of snow: red and white, blood on snow, boys and girls. *Martisor* was a happy occasion Annie had been eagerly expecting. It signalled the end of winter, even though, when she looked outside, she saw white land and blue sky and snow that seemed to rise toward the horizon and meet the cold, unmelting sun.

A long time ago, before he died, Samson had said that parents sent a stork to their children wherever they happened to be to convey their love and blessings on *martisor*. He had given Annie a silver coin from the old country the last March before his death, and she had since lost it or it had been taken away. Annie looked out the window while she stirred the mushrooms in the skillet. No stork appeared in the sky, flapping toward her window. What did it matter? She could have helped the teacher give so much pleasure to the young children, so much fun drawing and cutting out hearts and birds and flowers, all wishes for spring and a good life. Her regret was as much for them and the teacher, who she believed would regret her absence, as it was for herself.

No more school. After all those decades, it still surprised my mother that she hadn't protested. She had stared at the icons rather than look at Aunt Sophie whose eyes, severe as a saint's glare, watched for any sign of disobedience, the rolling pin shaking in her crossed arms. My mother shivered in the cold parlour, under the rack of cobalt blue dishes along one wall. She had grown to her full height of five foot three by then, still a few inches shorter and many pounds lighter than the expansive Sophie, whose breasts, my mother said, swelled to the size of a full cow's udder heavy with milk. Uncle Tudor had already departed for town, the children finished their breakfast, when Sophie pulled her into the parlour. Uncle Tudor would have done nothing to help her. The children, like cooking, collecting eggs, knitting and gutting chickens, were Sophie's business.

So, as she prepared the *ciorbă* according to Sophie's instructions, her aunt rattled and rustled in the upstairs bedrooms, changing the linens and turning over the mattresses, clacking the broom over the boards, rolling up the rugs to take outside for a dusting. Annie understood that she had reached the end of her stay in the household. As she drained the broth, the sapped vegetables to be kept for the pigs, she decided to run away. She mixed a bit of flour in water to make a paste, then added it to the broth, along with the mushrooms, which had sautéed to the right consistency and colour. Sophie had taught her well. Annie added just enough sauerkraut brine to sour the soup, ordinarily something Sophie would have done with fermented bran, but she had none left. Not today, she wouldn't leave today; such a decision required getting used to, some forethought, some choice of possessions to take. She could carry her few belongings in a box or cardboard suitcase. She would be neither flummoxed nor delayed by excess.

Tenka had mailed a postcard, brought home just last week by Uncle Tudor from the Dysart post office. Married now to a house painter, living in Regina, she wrote that she was well and hoped that Annie was the same. She hadn't seen Tenka or spoken to her sister since Montana, had not even known about the marriage until the postcard arrived. It had not been given to her directly. Annie knew of its existence only because she overheard Uncle reading it to Sophie, although the card was addressed to Annie, care of her uncle and general delivery in Dysart. They talked about her sister Tenka. Respectful of His Majesty's Royal Mail, Sophie kept all letters, cards and bills in the drawer at the bottom of the dish cupboard in the cold parlour. At the risk of a vicious beating, Annie found the postcard—what did she care if Aunt discovered her going through all these papers? She was only searching for what belonged to her. Why would Aunt Sophie keep news of her sister Tenka a secret? Why would she not let Annie read her own mail?

Perhaps John and Nick also received cards—she didn't know, as John now rarely went to school, and Nick had left Montana a while back, she had also heard, perhaps running away. What her big brother had done, she would do. She did not know where Nick was now living. Unlike Tenka, he had not thought to send his beloved sister a card. But how would she get in touch with John before she ran away? Nothing she said to him at school, nothing she did for him—like completing arithmetic homework in the schoolyard before Teacher clanged the cowbell and classes began or offering him pieces of *plăcintă*—made him smile. Whenever she talked to him, John turned his face away as if looking for something, or hearing someone, far away in the distance. He shifted from one foot to the next, my mother unable to remember John ever standing or sitting still for two moments together. And Mary? Where was her sister Mary? Tenka must know, and Tenka would welcome her baby sister Annie with open arms. Together they'd walk the rich and glittering streets of Regina the Queen City, fine enough for Marie of Romania if only she would deign to come, the city of countless streets, many of which were paved. Sophie's brutality would melt away from Annie's life like icicles in the spring.

Snow blown by the wind into high drifts pushed against the sides of the house and the farm buildings, the sun obliterated by the flurry of flakes whirling through the sky. On a day like today, she would have walked holding one or two of the younger children by the hand, heads bent, scarves wrapped up to their noses, and arrived home coated with snow like ghosts emerging out of the snowbound landscape. Eva would miss her, and she would miss Eva, whom she had never blamed for Sophie's predations. She used to pull Eva across the frozen slough on two planks her uncle had secured together, then mounted on sawed-off cutter blades. They had pretended they were being chased by ravening wolves in the shape of her other cousins, scurrying and scuttling and slipping on the ice, howling the way wolves howled in their imagination.

Her grief over the loss of school was mollified somewhat by news of Tenka and by the growing sense that she was about to begin a new kind of life very soon, one that not even Sophie could prevent. Not even a slap against the back of her head, almost knocking her into the soup pot, diminished the dream. What were you doing, stupid girl? Sophie could hit and insult as much as she pleased now, and, yes, Annie had been daydreaming over the stove, a dangerous and stupid lapse of attention for a good cook. Dreams did not season the stew. Sophie was too pre-occupied with other matters to pursue the attack. She told Annie to wipe the table before setting out the soup bowls, wide and more flat than deep for *ciorbă*. Aunt tasted the soup and regarded Annie suspiciously when she could find no fault, as if some demon had stepped into her kitchen to help the orphan.

Noticing the cleaver on the sideboard next to the sink, the very one she had used to chop vegetables for the *ciorbă*, Annie picked it up, turned toward Sophie and held it tightly against her breast like an archangel's sword. With all the righteous force and fury of a fourteen-year-old, Annie decided that she would never fear this woman again nor let Aunt Sophie raise a hand against her again. Sophie crossed herself in the Orthodox style, muttering words Annie could not hear, then snorted *Devil, devil, devil!* and trundled out of the kitchen.

Stunningly easy. Her mind lifting as high as the prairie sky, Annie began singing a *doină*. She didn't know whether she could have used the cleaver or not. Perhaps she regretted the fact that Sophie never so much as touched her again after that day. Either the opportunity did not present itself or the desire was somehow suppressed, but Annie never experienced the pleasure of causing her aunt physical pain. Swearing vengeance at such a young age, she never forgot. In not forgetting, she held on to the moral ferocity of the unforgiving. Hearing the news of her aunt's death, my mother enjoyed the dubious pleasure, at last, of saying "God is Great." She did not attend the funeral.

The blow to the head stirred a kind of chronic, low-lying headache that Annie first experienced after the accident with the horse. Although healed, her eye remained skewed, and Annie became prone to long bouts of piercing pain behind the eye that only darkness and quiet would ease. In a household of many people, little privacy, crowded rooms, endless chores and regular beatings, little opportunity existed for a restful cure. She never mentioned the pain to her aunt, who would only have shrugged it off or compared it to her own headaches, a kind of cosmic metaphor Aunt employed to describe the work she had to do, work without end for which she received no credit, not to mention the anxiety-ridden presence of the orphaned girl in her house. Annie did learn, however, to keep secret what troubled her, to endure pain rather than to reveal plans, useful knowledge in one's quest for survival.

The snow lay as high as prison walls, but it was not made of stone. What had fallen could be ploughed through one way or another. The temperature was not so cold that it would freeze the skin of her cheeks and the breath in her lungs. If it was, she knew how to breathe in sub-zero weather and how to protect her face. She would not be found frozen like a cow in the middle of the field or a poor, wandering man befuddled by the blizzard and trudging blindly into the depths of a ditch, freezing to death. Wagon and truck wheels had ridged and flattened out pathways on the road. Uncle had experienced little difficulty. The walk to the Dysart train station did not exceed three miles. A child of the prairies, Annie was also a child of winter, a season that energized rather than disheartened her. Accustomed to extremes, my mother detested the torpor of summer more than she loathed the cold of winter.

In little more than a week, it would be All Saints' Day, and the family planned to attend church services. Annie would stay home and cook *mucenic*, everyone's favourite food for the celebration of the holy martyrs (*mucenici*) of the Orthodox faith. The challenge lay in getting to the train station unnoticed by anyone she knew—not an easy task in a small village—just as the train was about to leave. It was possible to purchase a ticket to Regina from the conductor on board, thereby bypassing the ticket agent entirely. How much money would she need? How much had she hoarded in her Queen Alexandra tin? She knew where Sophie kept a little black change purse under her girdle in the top drawer of her bedroom dresser, bulky with coins and dollar bills rolled up like pencils, watched over by the unnerving eyes of Saint Monica. After counting, withdrawing or depositing money, Sophie snapped the purse shut like the jaws of a turtle. Annie gasped at the possibility of theft. To steal money from Aunt Sophie! The audacity made her blood run cold, and she felt the way she did when the boys stuffed snow down the back of her coat. If Aunt Sophie discovered her, not even Annie could imagine the punishment or the weapon Sophie would choose.

Ignoring her headache, she collected the wide bowls from the cupboard and stacked them at one end of the table. She would not arrange them until the children arrived home, and they would of course wait for Uncle to come out of one of the farm sheds, where he performed one winter task or another, before they ate. In addition to *ciorbă*, they would eat bread baked that morning and spiced sausages. The kitchen steamed with the moist fragrances of simmering spices and tangy soup. Always hungry, Annie rubbed her stomach, careful to hide the action from Sophie, lest the woman, seeing desire, deprived her niece of satisfaction. Oh, Sophie knew very little about what Annie really thought. Looking at the hairnetted woman, her button eyes stuck under heavy brows, her hips broad and hard, her feet in carpet slippers and wool socks, Annie cringed as if experiencing once again every blow Sophie had struck, every slash with belt or broom, every deprivation and humiliation.

God was not going to get Annie to the train on time if she did not use her wits. Should she write to Tenka first, now that she knew the address, or find her way from the Regina station somehow to the street where her sister lived? She could hide the letter and mail it secretly. Occasionally Uncle sent her to the post office to mail his own correspondence and bills, saying she could keep a nickel for herself if she went alone, or two nickels for herself and Eva. Those nickels had mounted up over the past three years; the sum just needed a bit of bolstering with money from Sophie's change purse. Annie would have to withdraw a small, perhaps unnoticeable, amount at the last possible moment before Sophie had a chance to notice the loss.

So, the festival of the saints seemed the best moment, a church-dominated celebration when she would be left alone in the house, with time enough to steal cash and steal away. At least Annie had a point of reference, a specific address, a beloved sister to shelter her. Annie simply did not think of running toward a great city like New York or London or Paris or even Toronto. Looking for neither adventure nor freedom, she chose familiarity and love, embodied in Tenka, who just happened to be living in Regina. The city, however interesting and enticing, came second to the person. If Tenka had sent Annie a card from Bucharest, my mother believed that somehow she would have managed to reach her sister there. Having made the decision, she was determined to leave. She would take the next few days to look over what clothes she could pack and how best to pack them. She did not wish to be encumbered with luggage on the walk to the train station. Passengers could board a train bound for Regina at an hour when virtually all the Romanians in town would be attending the All Saints' Day mass on March 9.

After the service, a feast in the church hall, and Sophie never missed a Romanian feast dinner, especially when she herself prepared one or more of the main dishes in quantities that would have exhausted many a lesser woman. To receive compliments on the excellence of her cuisine placed Sophie on a cloud of self-congratulation. The fact that Annie did as much in the preparation of the meals was a bit of information Sophie never cared to divulge. Already, Sophie had prepared a list of the ingredients required for her contribution to the church dinner besides the standard *mucenic*, which every other Romanian woman had offered to bring to the dinner. Sophie wanted to prepare a main course. Annie could make *mucenic* for the children. What household would not have dozens of the sweet pieces of pasta shaped in the figure eight? Sophie's vanity meant the entire family would stay at the hall until she decided it was time to leave, once everyone had tasted her food. All the bowls had to be emptied before they departed. There was no reason for anyone to return home before Annie had packed, walked to the train station, boarded the train and turned her back on Dysart. The soup was good, Sophie said, congratulating herself rather than Annie. After all, the niece had only followed the aunt's recipe.

A strong girl with good legs despite her small size, Annie was not daunted by the long walk and haul over a snow-covered, treacherously slippery road. There was no guarantee another blizzard wouldn't blind and block the way. She concentrated on immediate problems, rather than worrying herself about potential hazards. During the next week, she helped her aunt in the kitchen, dressed the children for school, swept the floors, beat the rugs, wrung out the laundry, fed the chickens and decided on which two dresses she would take, in addition to the dress she wore. She would also pack her Queen Alexandra tin with food because she didn't know how long the journey would last and did not want to spend money on food along the way. She would be more adventurous in raiding the pantry this time.

Sophie scarcely spoke to my mother that last week, as if she sensed the resistance in Annie's soul. With a new baby and young children still underfoot, with the preparations for the All Saints' Day feast, she relied on her niece to help in the kitchen and look after the children, never raising a hand. Sophie perhaps believed that she herself was in peril if she assaulted the child one more time. Unequal battles were one thing if victory was assured; confronting the rage of an opponent who now looked as if she could give back as good as she got was quite another. Sophie issued instructions but stayed her hand.

On the day of the service and feast, Uncle carried covered bowls and pans of food to his car. He planned to drive to the church hall first, to deposit the goods, taking the oldest children with him. There was not enough room for the entire brood to go at one time. While Sophie scrubbed the younger children and chose their clothes for them, Annie remained in the kitchen, having kneaded the dough earlier. Not a complicated dish, *mucenic* requires dexterity rather than sweat. The ball of dough was now rising in a covered brown bowl. She ground walnuts with cinnamon sticks and sugar. Given the demand, the local grocer in Dysart had stocked sufficient supply of the expensive ingredients. On the stove a large pot of water was boiling, to which Annie added honey. The dough ready, she removed it from the bowl, punched it down and began rolling it over the flour-covered surface of the table. Sophie stepped into the kitchen carrying a swaddled, bonneted baby, stared at her niece but said nothing.

Annie cut lengths the width of a rope, just long enough for each to ring her forefinger. She made dozens, lost in the pleasure of the touch and smell of dough and honey and cinnamon. Then she shaped two ropes at a time into circles and gently pinched them together into figure eights. Why eight, rather than six, she did not know, although the number was supposedly related to the holy saints who were being celebrated that day in church. She had heard references now and then to the forty martyrs, so perhaps eight, which easily divided into forty, had something to do with that. If the Devil himself had stood in the door of the kitchen, she would have ignored him, for she felt as close to blissful as she had felt since living on her father's farm. She raised her head to return Sophie's stare and her aunt retreated.

Samson had told his children about Sfântul Ilie, who had some responsibility for thunder and lightning and medicinal plants. Tată also said that Ilie caused every great fire in the scorching heat of summer. And Annie stood by the table, several figure eights in the palm of her hand, she remembered a horizon of flame racing toward their sod house years ago, and Tată grabbing the children and Tinca gathering as many clothes and blankets as she could carry. Was the saint behind that wall of flame and smoke, the grass of the prairie crackling, the wind hot and ashy, blowing heat over their faces? She remembered sitting on Tată's shoulder, as if he was about to dance the *horă*. He waded into the middle of the slough, the children hanging on to his coat and to each other, and the flames, like a legion of frenetic devils, leaped and hopped, fizzled and roared across the land. Their house had not been burned during the prairie fire, although she knew it had rolled over the thatched roofs of other houses of people who had also found refuge in the waters of the sloughs.

Into the pot of sweetened water she dropped the figure eights and waited until they rose to the top, a sign that they had cooked to the proper consistency. One can add the walnut mixture to the pot at this time after removing it from the heat, or one can scoop out the cooked figures and baste them with the sweet, nutty paste. My mother stirred the paste into the pot and let the soup rest before gently pouring it out into another bowl, which she placed in the icebox. A delicious treat for all the children, who could never eat enough of the pretzels, no matter how many they consumed in the church hall. Proud of her knowledge and skill, my mother believed that even the witch Sophie would have approved of her efforts and, jealous of the success, resented her culinary expertise. Despite her fears, Annie felt like singing that day as she watched the family crowd themselves into Uncle's car after he returned from the church hall and disappear down the lane onto the grid road.

Removing the apron and hanging it on the back of the kitchen door, she leaped up the stairs and from under her bed pulled out the wooden egg crate that she had lined with the brown paper Sophie kept in the larder for baking. In it she packed her two dresses, socks, underwear and her Queen Alexandra tin, now filled with sausages and cold cheese *plăcintă*, nuts and raisins and cheddar cheese. Precious little time remained to think about what she was doing. Then she entered Sophie's room, which smelled of candlewax and the lye her aunt used in the washing. Every day Sophie lighted the candles in front of her icons and prayed for the return of her beads. Surprising to my mother, Sophie had not stormed through the household on discovering their disappearance. She heard Sophie tell Uncle that perhaps she had inadvertently left them behind in the church or the hall.

Finding the change purse under the girdle that Sophie hooked and laced and tightened around her torso only when she wasn't pregnant, Annie took two of the four rolls and several coins, which, added to her store of nickels, she believed would be enough to get her to Regina and her beloved Tenka's house. Can one steal from the Devil? Can one rob a witch? Years later, to salve her conscience, she sent Sophie a Christmas card with a five-dollar bill.

Dressing for the cold, she shut the front door behind her. With the crate in her arms, she began the long trek to the train station. The sky was blowing icy blue that day, a cold that licked and tingled her cheeks. All the way to the village, the distant elevators in view almost from the beginning, she sang to herself, trying to hold back the terror creeping like the cold into her mind. Her arms weary, she felt fear push her forward. Sophie's house sank behind a snow-drifted rise in the land. Unlike Lot's unfortunate wife, my mother did not glance back.

Part Four

Răcituri (Jellied Pork Hocks)

4 pork hocks
1 teaspoon salt
3 garlic cloves
14–16 cups water
paprika

- *Place pork hocks in a pot and cover with water.*
- *Bring to boil and simmer for 15 minutes. Drain pork hocks, rinse and place in a large pot.*
- *Add 14–16 cups water (or enough to fill pot just over halfway) and add salt.*
- *Bring to boil and simmer, skimming off any foam that forms on top, for 3 to 4 hours until meat falls from bones.*
- *Crush garlic cloves and add to pot during last half-hour of cooking.*
- *Remove bones and discard. Scoop out meat and place in individual bowls or large serving bowl.*
- *Strain broth and pour over meat.*
- *Place in refrigerator to set for a few hours or overnight.*

- *Remove any fat that has settled on top before unmoulding onto serving plate.*
- *Sprinkle with paprika.*

Serves 6.

CHAPTER 16

We soon believe what we desire.

My mother was never a teenager; if the concept had been invented, no one bothered to inform Annie. Although she experienced the dizzying and frenetic hormonal changes of any teenager, she was not influenced by either the advertising or the psychological industries that later sanctioned, perhaps created, the adolescent mentality. Still very close to her peasant roots and Transylvanian heritage, she experienced no impact of the Jazz Age and American cinema on her early life. Although the RCMP impounded an illegal Romanian still in the Dysart area during the Prohibition years, she had little awareness of bootlegging or the complicated relations between Ottawa and the provinces. Limited in her grasp of history and politics, she understood nothing of the implications and consequences of the Versailles peace talks in 1919 in which the legendary Queen Marie of Romania had participated. Although taught their names in school, she could not name the Canadian prime ministers and had to be reminded during the early years of the Depression who R. B. Bennett was.

The great intellectual forces of Modernism did not brush against her consciousness. Enthralled by imaginative narratives when a public school pupil, she did not read novels, or any books, as a young woman. She was a member of the last generation in

Canadian history whose childhood passed without benefit of regular radio transmission, billboards, electronic imagery, motorized traffic jams, white noise and American film. An airplane flying over the prairies just after the First World War would have been a sight to behold. She beheld none. Annie did remember seeing one movie, a silent feature shown in a Regina movie house in 1928, and thought the images odd, the flickering characters moving and gesticulating in ways real people did not, their mouths opening like fish sucking after food in a tank. The romance of the silver screen failed on the spot.

Living too much in her own mind, and searching always for a kind of lost love, Annie found it difficult to imagine someone else's life or to stop mulling over what she had lost. Taken out of school at an early age, she lamented the fact. A love of stories became entangled with personal sorrow, anxiety about the future and a superstitious apprehension of the world. She required a school building's formal structure and a teacher's organization of information to support her nebulous yearning for knowledge. Without those, her intellectual foundations collapsed. She did not develop the self-regard of the autodidact because, once severed from school, she made no attempt to reconstruct her intellectual life. It wasn't easy to pick up a book when learning had been so blatantly despised. The contempt in the repeated question, what did she need with an education? infected her bloodstream like a virus. What Sophie had despised and possibly feared, being unlettered herself, Annie internalized. Beatings injured the intellect, perhaps beyond the point of full recuperation.

Although she regretted the lack of schooling all her life, Annie never thought of herself as stupid, despite Sophie's massive propaganda campaign to the contrary. Feeling worthless at times, she knew that she had been valued in her father's eyes.

That memory helped shore up the foundations of her self-esteem so relentlessly battered by her aunt. Her native intelligence, seeking roots in the undernourished soil of her brain, also survived, expressing itself in reconstructed memories, in the complicated manipulations of knitting and crocheting, the results of which, never copied from precut patterns, defy analysis. Patronized as mere feminine craft, her work with needle and thread originated in mind and purpose, in design and vision, signs of a living intelligence. Once she held up a doily and exclaimed, "Look, I've crocheted a blizzard!"

In the culinary realm, her expertise was so rich that no one could successfully imitate her cooking. In developing a sense of her own desires and needs, without a strong intelligence she could have lost herself in mere brutishness and rancour. What Annie would have achieved, like so many abused people, had she been allowed to pursue formal studies, remains a matter of conjecture. She never did fully recognize her own particular talents for survival. Rather than sink into dismal anonymity, beaten into semi-bovine stupor by her aunt, Annie overcame fear and took a step out.

As she carefully tapped a hammer against a clay pot of her indestructible sanseveria, she offered instruction: A plant outgrows its home and it needs to be transplanted into something just a bit larger. With this plant (she called it by the common, abusive name of mother-in-law's tongue), one needs to break a pot to free the plant. Don't even think of disturbing it until the outward pressure of its compacted and strangled roots in the depleted soil has cracked the pot. Understanding the needs of a plant was the key to success. Annie never spoke in technical, professional terms about anything she grew, relying on folklore and practical experience rather than horticultural science. If she didn't know the actual facts, she often pretended she did, so as not to give anyone the advantage. Without explaining how, she knew why her impressive hoya, which she mistakenly called the honey plant because its waxy flowers dripped nectar, blossomed every year when similar plants in other houses failed to bloom. "I just know," she used to say, understanding when to leave the plant alone and when to do something drastic.

Her achievement in leaving her aunt's home was large. A small girl, scarcely out of childhood, feeling the strength of her legs, she walked toward her freedom under the infinite sky. When she arrived in Regina, she did not think of returning to school, nor did she think about freedom and independence. She thought of reunification with her beloved sister, thought of somehow re-establishing the family she had lost years earlier after the death of her father. Restricted by her own perceptions of relationships, Annie assumed that once scattered for several years, a family could ultimately continue where it left off before the diaspora. Relying too much on the biological connection, she believed the intervening years would have had little or no effect on emotions.

Freedom was an abstract, essentially alien concept, but family love was real and tangible. Without family, she believed herself insignificant. Her identity depended on reciprocal love. No woman she had ever known existed outside of family responsibilities. Annie sometimes imagined a different kind of life elsewhere, living under better circumstances. The narratives of her early school years suggested that a wonderful world existed just beyond her reach, but the memory of her lost family irrevocably determined her choices.

Clicking with grasshoppers in the late summer, Regina was a new and prosperous city of many thousands of people in the 1920s, built literally on buffalo killing grounds around the river, the pile of animal bones providing its name Wascana. The meat was crucial to Native survival, the hides cleaned and stretched on the flat land for drying. Completed in 1919, the pseudo-Renaissance-styled legislative building rose in the middle of developing parkland, eventually to become one of the largest downtown parks of North America. Breathless, Annie got off the train and found her way outside the station, astounded by the clangour of electric streetcars. The sound of hammers and drills echoed in the air. When she saw it a few days later, the neo-classical immensity of the Radisson Plaza Hotel, still under construction, appeared like a monumental temple to ancient gods on the prairie landscape.

Moreover, department stores, incomparably greater than any village store, stuffed with goods from all over the world, stores like R. H. Williams on the corner of Hamilton and 11th Avenue, and Sherwood Department Store at Albert and Victoria, could satisfy any of her material desires. The Williams store would eventually become a Simpson's department store and began my mother's lifelong love affair with catalogue shopping, first from Simpson's, then Eaton's. Need for an item was not as great as desire and the simple pleasure of possession. Having little, she desired much. Attaining much, she ordered more. In later life, Annie's closets and dresser drawers became storehouses of unopened packages. When the financial means became available, she tried to cushion herself with supplies and never feel want again, the pots of gold at the end of so many fairy tales becoming undergarments and bedsheets. This acquisition of material goods revealed an uneasy, dissatisfied and unfulfilled heart.

Experiencing the Depression as a very young woman, she hoarded as a mature adult. Looking at her overstocked cupboards and closets, Annie saw want staring her in the face. Today a casino, the Union Depot where Annie disembarked from the train had opened in 1912 and confirmed her belief that Regina was a kind of magical city. If she quickly saw that the streets had not been paved with proverbial gold, she nonetheless did not walk on mud or dust. And so many people. Born in a region of a few hundred immigrants surrounded by the eternity of prairie, she was startled, even initially frightened, by the legions of people. Annie was not accustomed to strangers and never felt comfortable with people she didn't know.

Among them was a considerable population of Romanians, original immigrants and their children, who founded St. Nicholas in 1901, the first Romanian Orthodox church in Saskatchewan, scarcely a generation after the last pile of buffalo bones by the Wascana River. Her own uncle Simeon had attended services there well before his brother Samson boarded the ship in Antwerp. Many Romanians also laboured in the construction of the legislative building overlooking the lake. Tenka and her husband lived on Reynolds Street. Asking directions outside the train station to her sister's street, holding the crate like a shield against her body, Annie was not culturally isolated.

Many people in this wonderful, electrified city spoke her language and understood her customs. With the prairie in her eyes, the family in her heart, Byzantium in her soul, by running away from Sophie's home, Annie had not left her heritage far behind. She was accustomed to walking over rough terrain and carrying burdens should the need arise. Her peasant blood came to the rescue. And walked she did, her feet warm in two pairs of her uncle's hand-knitted wool socks, which she had wisely chosen to steal and wear that morning. She had often washed and stretched them on wire sock holders to help them keep their size and shape. Wool was prone to shrinking.

March is a month of many contradictory personalities, so one could never trust the weather. Sunny and warm one day, a belting blizzard the next, icicles melting, nose hairs freezing.

Unlike the snow in Dysart, the snow in Regina piled grey and uninviting along the sides of the roads. She had other things on her mind besides playing in the snowy fields with her cousins. As she carried the egg crate filled with her possessions, walking toward a sister she hadn't seen in five years and who was married to a man Annie had never met, Annie wondered whether Tenka would be pleased to see her.

Astonished herself that she had found the courage to leave Sophie's household and stifle her fears sufficiently to mount the steps and enter the belly of the locomotive, she had cried as the train began its rumbling crawl out of the Dysart station. There's a Romanian superstition about a small bird flying into the house. It presages someone's death. My mother told me she felt like the bird that day as she cried on the train. Telling the story, she twisted her lacy handkerchief and compared her frightened, youthful self to a bird panic-stricken in a house, bewildered by the sudden veering of walls against which it beat its wings.

The blocks of streets logically laid out, early Regina did not confuse the newcomer with curves and culs-de-sac. Within walking distance from the station, Reynolds Street was broken in half by railway tracks. Tenka lived on the south side, just above Victoria Avenue. Annie had little difficulty locating her sister's home, unprepossessing in appearance, but to Annie's mind a palace out of *The Arabian Nights*. She did not expect to find caves glistening with rubies and emeralds, or magical doors, or viziers with scimitars, or powerful genies whispering inside their lamps. She found her beloved Tenka, who, when she opened the door, did not immediately embrace her sister. "Ana!" she exclaimed, pronouncing the Romanian birth name by which she had always called my mother during their childhood days together. Fatigued from the train journey, her arms weary from carrying the crate, her mouth dry from nerves and her heart about to shatter, Annie for one brief moment doubted that she would be welcomed. Her knees weakened, and she collapsed on the threshold.

Her sister did in fact welcome Annie, the way an adult welcomes but remains cautious with an unfamiliar relative. Annie never quite understood that Tenka had matured way beyond her years, a married woman now expecting her first child, her love no longer exclusively focused on her youngest sister. Times had moved on, times had changed. Tenka lived in a modern city with conveniences, not on the farm with an outhouse, and unlike Annie she had put the death of her father behind her. Tenka did not fully comprehend the horror of domestic brutality that had marked Annie's life for several years. Listening to what Annie described about her life with Sophie, she did not dwell on the story and showed little understanding of her sister's psychology. Even if she had, she would not have been capable of fulfilling Annie's bottomless need for assurance. Tenka's duties were clear and divided. Not seeing the world through a child's eyes or with a child's nostalgia for a quasi-mythical past, she had found a job before she married in Regina and now looked toward the future in a very well kept home. You could eat off the floors of her house, Annie said with some pride, a virtue she herself emulated. An odd expression, when a clean table must always be preferable to a floor. A good woman, Tenka received her sister politely and affectionately. Her husband did not object. To her lasting credit, she offered the orphaned runaway a home for as long as she could. Annie, disappointed in her sister ultimately, remained nonetheless grateful.

For the first few weeks, until she settled herself, which meant sorting out her feelings and fighting back waves of anxiety—suppose Sophie sent the RCMP after her? suppose she was forced to return to the farm?—Annie wandered the streets of Regina. She discovered the Wascana River and the legislature, the downtown core. She saw groups of Native people walking in long coats with their heads bowed, averting their eyes to avoid any direct visual contact, reminding her of the itinerant workers in the Dysart area. When she tried to speak to them, they acknowledged her politely but did not engage in conversation. Ever a quiet people, they revealed little of their thoughts.

Sophie did not pursue her niece; she never even inquired as to her whereabouts although she knew perfectly well where Tenka lived and could only have surmised that Annie had left for her sister's place. No one in the family searched for Annie or sent a note to her Reynolds Street address. As Sophie's children grew up, Annie disappeared largely from their collective memory, as if she had never lived in their house. When communication was re-established decades later, her suffering remained unacknowledged. During all the many years of separation, the inexorably silent Sophie never apologized for her behaviour. From Sophie, Annie also learned the usefulness and the consequences of a lifetime of silence. When she chose to deny aspects of her life, her silence clamped down like a tomb's lid over her memory, not without her paying a heavy price. Secrecy worries the mind and corrodes the character.

Neither a child nor an adult, certainly not a modern teenager, my mother needed to find work. Although not impoverished, Tenka and George were not rich, and the baby would make demands on what income they enjoyed. Annie began to feel guilty for living in the household without contributing her share to its costs. She cleaned, for Sophie had also taught her niece the craft of cleaning—scouring would be a more accurate word. Once she tied up her hair in a kerchief and grabbed a mop, a Romanian woman set about cleaning with a concentrated commitment that spelled doom for anyone who got in her way or stepped on her recently polished floors before she had a chance to cover them with newspaper. A brush whose bristles had not been worn down bespoke a lackadaisical attitude to scrubbing.

On the farm Annie had learned to raise and decapitate chickens or snap their necks with a flick of the wrist, to pluck and singe their feathers, to plant seeds and cultivate a vegetable garden, to plough the field, to pull a cow's teats effortlessly without getting kicked in the side by a hind hoof, to sew, knit and crochet, to prevent a sow from eating her litter, to bake bread and *plăcintă*, to prepare soups and stews and *mămăligă*, to sing praises to God in church, to pickle and preserve a wide range of foods, to wash laundry by hand and wring it out with the mangle, to iron with heated flatirons without scorching the cloth (she had done so once, and the belt had broken the skin on her back). She could also care for young children, boil their diapers, apply ointment to rashes on their bums, soothe their colic and make them giggle in her arms. In Regina there was little need for yet another farm girl, but work was to be had for the asking. Before the Depression, many a woman advertised for domestic help. Perfectly qualified to clean another person's dirt and care for another person's children, Annie found the first of her several jobs as a housekeeper.

Although she was not well paid, and was paid progressively less each year of the Depression for the long and hard work, housekeeping taught my mother many things about running a messy and complicated household. It also deepened the depressions that plagued her for most of her life. Putting one's arm into a toilet bowl did not engender high spirits. Although she was happy to give Tenka most of what she earned, despair threatened to knock her off her feet. The first few happy weeks in Regina collapsed, and the frightfulness of her situation began to trouble my mother. The city offered many visual distractions, buildings standing higher than the grain elevators in Dysart. Anyone's dream could easily develop and grow here. Annie could not help believing that something more should be happening in her life, that the void in her heart, soon to be filled with the memorable stone, demanded more than she now had to make her feel less alone, less anxious, less fearful that whatever she was doing, no matter how well she did it, failed to provide solace.

The large and noisy city was invaded by grasshoppers in the summer, blasted by snowy winds in the winter. There were wonderful shops, but she walked the streets as if stepping through a mirage. Her belief that something terrible would happen intensified. Perhaps her state of mind was nothing more than the peasant reluctance to believe in good fortune without paying a price, for the Devil was behind the cross or in the stone pile; perhaps it was her own sense of dislocation. Her body uncomfortable and twitching in whatever clothes she wore, Annie sought distraction to save herself from despair. It was hard to hold back the tears some days, but she did. It was even harder to move her body, sapped of energy and desire, but Annie moved. If hope did not change the weather, neither did self-pity. The work at hand distracted the heart, and she willed herself into activity and patience, but on many days her body didn't seem to be inside her own clothes.

Rejoining her sister, Annie began developing feelings of separateness and isolation. To some degree, she was younger than her years, unlike Tenka, who was older than her nineteen. Strangely, Annie found her sister's home crowded, even after living in Aunt Sophie's packed household. Her sense of disappointment translated into lack of space. There was no room in more than the physical sense. Her brothers John and Nick and her sister Mary, although she would see each one of them within the next few years, never re-established the original family. When Annie could bring herself to talk about it, depression was a congealing of the blood in her arteries, a closing of her mind as it froze like ice over the prairie sloughs. She could feel the chill about her heart, and it was so easy to give in, so tempting.

At the darkest hours, her heart went cold, and the young girl of fifteen often asked herself why she should wake up from one day to the next. That she placed one foot in front of the other and forced herself to complete the tasks of the day saved Annie from spiralling downward into a crippling despair. If she willed herself into believing that one day she would receive what she desired, she could crack through the ice, breathe and survive. What she desired, though, remained nebulous, mired in a myth of family, ill-defined, distorted by her nostalgia for the past. Nor did she know how to go about acquiring it, as it lay beyond reach, like the peak of a glass mountain. Without guidance or help, she dug deep into her own self and intuitively grasped on to she knew. She remembered her father's dancing and she thought of the garden. Remembered cabbages and beans, fancifully imagining her father's spirit playing the *tilinca* among the rows of perfectly hoed vegetables. The garden always returned, she kept repeating to herself, if one only worked at it, every spring and summer, regardless of the severity of the winter. Never an optimist under the best of circumstances, Annie nonetheless hung on to an image of herself among the cabbages, which offered her surprising beauty and comfort. As an old woman scarcely able to stand, to sit among flowers in the yard remained her last joy.

She did not stand still to freeze to death in her depression. Spring would come and she would hill the potatoes or stake the tomatoes and pluck fat beets out of the earth to make a splendid borscht. Even in Regina. After days, sometimes weeks, the depression thawed, leaving her body worn and weary, for severe depression is as physical as it is psychological. Like a stone lifted off my heart, she said. A calm and not spectacular hope flowed once more like the run-off in spring.

CHAPTER 17

He that labours and thrives spins gold.

Canadian children in the first decades of the twentieth century, like children in many parts of the world, constituted a cheap and largely unprotected labour force. Life was physically harder and potentially dangerous on the farm, although not demeaning. Annie never resented the actual chores. Despite Sophie's outbursts—so fierce they bring to mind the Romanian saying, "Anger is a brief madness"—Annie loved the agricultural life, finding both release and joy in the fields and the garden. Work as a house cleaner in Regina came closer to destroying her soul. Not the nature of the work itself, but the fact that she did it in a home that belonged to someone else.

During this time Tenka received a postcard photograph of brother John standing proud in a military uniform. He had run away from home in Dysart and joined the army, as the picture taken in the late twenties would attest. Except he had joined not the army but the reformed First Regina Regiment, reorganized in 1924 to include civilian volunteers who met for various exercises and drills. This organization could have provided him with a sense of purpose, certainly camaraderie; instead, it provided only a temporary distraction from the restlessness from which he clearly suffered as much as his sister. Annie was proud of John and even believed for a time that he would soon see military action somewhere in the world. That was not the case and never would be. If John had run away to see the world, he was stopped short in his tracks in more ways than the metaphorical. She missed her brother dreadfully, a feeling compounded by a vague sense of guilt because she believed she had not helped him enough in Dysart, had not convinced him that the family would one day be restored and they would all live together again.

Through Tenka Annie also learned that her oldest brother, Nick, having left Montana, worked in a meat packing plant in Vancouver for a while before returning to Saskatchewan to marry and begin a family in Truax. She should have been happy for her brothers. In a way she was, but she knew that like Tenka, the boys had also moved beyond her dream of reuniting the family. Both John and Nick had made decisions that removed Annie from their lives. Happy for them as she wore down the bristles of her scrub brushes, she understood that she had lost them. She envied their ability to make choices and live new lives, even as she needed their physical presence and hungered for a transforming event in her own.

Low-lying depression clouded her spirits like mud stirred up from the bottom of a slough. Christmas and Easter, festive and colourful holidays, were always observed in her sister's household. She would stretch dough over the kitchen table, roast lamb and colour Easter eggs in her sister's household, but however evident her skill, her heart was absent. She reminded herself of her wretched life in Sophie's house and tried to believe that happiness lay at her fingertips. Annie attended the Romanian Orthodox church in Regina, but found her mind wandering away from the priest's sermons, her singing responses mere rote, the words and music as lovely and hollow as a decorated Easter egg whose flesh had been blown out of the shell. The icons became pieces of painted wood rather than symbols of

divine love. Taking Communion, Annie did not absorb meaning, did not feel spiritually enriched. Her religious convictions
waned. What did the priest know? He was only a man himself,
and she distrusted his authority, began to dislike all priests.
Attendance at church did not lift her out of the muck of melancholy, a feeling always present, even on the days when she
laughed and fingered the linens in department stores.

Not that Annie ever acquired the courage of atheism, for she
maintained a slender connection with the Church for many
decades. She ceased, though, to regard God as omnipotent and
caring. Her attitude to religion would always be compromised
by her personal experiences. Annie gave as much credence to the
Devil's influence as she did to God's benevolence.

She sank into a miasma of regret and sorrow, pulling herself
out only by the sheer necessity of getting down on her hands and
knees and scrubbing another woman's floors. Too young for the
consolations of philosophy, she relied on physical labour, con-
firming her undying notion that life consisted mostly of work,
pleasure being a temporary release from drudgery. At times she
pretended she was actually on her hands and knees between the
vegetables or she imagined a rose unfolding in the spread of
wash water over a flower-patterned linoleum. Imagination rendered actuality tolerable. Such had not always been the case, she
could still remember, for feasting and music wind about the
Romanian soul like flowering vines and flourished in her father's
house when he was alive.

Forgetting that her father had worked from dawn to dusk, like
every other immigrant, Annie remembered only the pleasures of
life on his farm. Her idea of the pleasures experienced there
became more and more distant, indistinct and mythologized by
the passage of time. What she meant by pleasure was the love of
her family, the boards of a table sagging under the weight of

food, a joyous dance encircling her beloved father. The circle, however, was broken. There was no longer a centre. All the distractions of a vibrant, new and burgeoning city did not rush in to fill the void.

Annie did not make friends easily. She knew many young people among the Romanian community but enjoyed no friendships, least of all the friendship of a young man. Shyness is often mistaken for coldness or indifference. From an early age, Annie was developing the protective armour of the abused and abandoned child. Her appearance and manner may have been off-putting. She wore Tenka's dresses, two sizes too large, until she could earn enough money to buy her own. Her black hair curled naturally, and she parted it in the middle so it hung down off her face like ruffled crow's wings. One eye slightly skewed, her front teeth overlapping, her smile more reticent than inviting, Annie often sat in the peasant woman's position of legs separated, feet flat on the floor, her lap ready to hold whatever bowl was necessary for the preparation of food. With deeply set dark eyes that could look hard and severe when not downcast, and unresponsive in public, she was not the belle of the Romanian ball.

Bypassed and ignored, she retreated into her own dissatisfied self. What she needed was a party, many parties, music and dance and casual excursions downtown with a group of like-minded friends. Reading would have expanded her view of the world and sharpened her perspective. Visiting the department stores to fondle their imported goods with her sister was a poor substitute. Loving laughter, suppressed in Sophie's house, she needed friends, needed to get out of her own defences. Longing to dance in a young man's arms, she had not learned any of the arts of enticement and sociability. Ironically, the contrast between what she had and who she was now pushed her farther away from people rather than closer. They assumed she wasn't interested. Her tremendous capacity to love furled its wings and hid its head in the cage of her heart.

Possessing the potential for excellence, she scanned the prairie sky over Regina on many a summer evening, the stars infinite in their plenitude and brilliant like fragments of diamond spangling a kerchief of deep blue silk. The city itself was not a sleepy backwater town: the Hotel Saskatchewan opened to the public in 1927, a symphony orchestra was founded in 1908 and the public library in 1909. Regina College, later a university, conducted classes. Partly benumbed by recurring bouts of depression, Annie did not entirely see what was before her eyes. The breadth of the sky, though, matched her yearning. As she observed Tenka and her husband with their infant daughter, Elaine, Annie turned in on herself and fought against a hardening, a sensation originating in disappointment. She didn't want to be cold—it wasn't really part of her nature—but the chill was covering her mind like the first snowfall over a wheat field. And she struggled against it, knowing how easy it was to succumb. If only she could have a garden, if only she could dig into the soil and plant a seed, if only she could have her own home and land.

There was, however, the baby. Sophie's fecundity had provided ample opportunity for my mother to understand the needs of the newborn. Looking after the child, she coddled, cradled, fed, sang Romanian nursery songs, played games and poured affection over the infant like holy oil. Here was a completely unthreatening, helpless and dependent, naturally affectionate creature who would not criticize or chastise, who responded happily to my mother's care. Annie would always be especially good with babies in the Romanian way, projecting her desire for family onto her sister's daughter. Moreover, understanding the fragile helplessness of a baby, she developed a sense of protectiveness toward the very young. Annie had it within her to fight to the death for her children, providing them with the protection missing from her own life.

She derived some satisfaction, therefore, from assisting her sister's family, some sense of worthiness re-established after spending a day scouring, washing by hand over a heavily ridged scrub board in a metal tub (for not every householder in the city had yet purchased an electric washing machine with a wringer attached). Now a collector's item and occasionally available for more money today than Annie earned in a year in Regina, their scrubbing surface sometimes made out of heavily ridged pool-green glass, scrub boards are a physical testimony to the history of women's work. Annie's arms ached and her hands turned red. Uncomplaining, she had done as much in Aunt Sophie's house. Happily, in Tenka's house, she was spared the abuse. She also earned a few dollars. The exhaustion of the body, the weariness of the spirit, were somewhat assuaged by her ability to work and to pay for her keep.

Every now and then, she found her way to the Union train station at Saskatchewan Drive and Broad Street, impressed by its square, creamy beige Tyndall limestone hauled from Manitoba. The Regina station saw the last train roll away in 1990. Very much in operation during her youth, it offered a gateway and exit, but she remained outside on the street, dreaming of the possibility of travelling east or west, the destination always vague. Romania, more and more fabulous in her mind, confused with her love for her father and his farm, beckoned, although she couldn't even begin to imagine how to get there. Neither intrepid by nature nor a victim of wanderlust, she didn't want to run away again; her sister's home provided her with refuge and shelter. The train, by its very existence, pointed in directions of alternatives and possibilities. Unarticulated discontent, psychological and sexual in origin, forestalled action. If she was torn between going and staying, the rip was temporary and easily mended. She stayed.

The train, though, had a profound influence on her family, as it did on many early Canadians. It not only carried her parents across the country, bringing her to Regina, but also provided a means by which her brother John would soon act out his own alienation and frustrations. Fed by the stories in school of travel and exotic adventures in foreign, legendary places, her imagination nonetheless derived nourishment from the Saskatchewan prairie. In many ways, the landscape was too large to escape, and her own blood had been mixed with the soil. Not a nomad at heart, having found a home where she was neither beaten nor despised, she still craved more experience and projected her longing onto the locomotive, as if iron, steam and rails could really satisfy her heart's desire.

Always entrepreneurial, a necessary virtue in the early days of settlement, Tenka's husband, George, moved his family into new quarters on Victoria Avenue in 1929, and he became a proprietor of a food store, Superior Grocery. To walk among the shelves loaded with tinned goods and a glass-covered counter displaying cuts of meat, to have a choice of food at one's fingertips, came very close to paradise for Annie. In her life, food became inextricably combined with love. The store became a tangible image of the ideal larder, the magical treasury of supplies, like Ali Baba's cave, except my mother was more interested in peaches and rutabaga than pearls and rubies. If one had cupboards and shelves well stocked with flour and tinned goods, well, then, one was armed against the predations of the world. In Annie's mind, food also expressed and guaranteed love. Look how delighted children were to eat what she had prepared.

Annie was happiest among the shelves, as any nutritionally deprived child would have been, until Tenka reminded her that the food was meant to sell, not to hoard or to consume at her pleasure. However correct, the admonition also served to remind Annie of her real status as a guest in someone else's domain. What she saw and touched did not truly belong to her. Permission was needed. Annie tried not to wallow in depression, a physically and psychologically exhausting procedure. No professional help or advice available, she was thrown onto her own devices to deal with states of mind she could scarcely understand. But she did learn how to prevent herself from slipping over the edge into total paralysis. What matter if she wept occasionally for reasons she could not define? There was work to be done. If done consistently and well, work salvaged the soul and saved the mind. From her childhood on, Annie became a living testament to the psychological and emotional necessity of work. Whatever dark thoughts dragged her spirits down, Romanian cooking, scrub boards and babies kept her head above the slough of despond.

Chapter 18

God makes the grass,
Satan sours the milk.

Where was he? How could she go to him? Just after the failure of the stock market in 1929, Tenka informed my mother that their brother John had slipped and fallen off a cattle car and cracked his head on the outside rail as the train rumbled by his bleeding body, by pure chance not decapitating him. They received the information from their brother Nick, now the father of two children, and they knew only what few words had been written in a note. John wasn't hospitalized in Regina, nor apparently anywhere close enough for his family to visit. For that matter, Annie had not been able to visit Nick. Not an impossible distance, the town of Truax was still too far away for a woman without means. Her sisters hadn't visited him either. Something wasn't working. Her brothers and sisters had grown up too quickly in her absence, too easily absorbed into new families and preoccupations. In a time of crisis, no one rushed to her brother's aid.

He had ever been reckless, ever restless, wandering from town to town after he had run away from his uncle's home in Dysart, always riding the rails to look for employment. The Depression compounded his difficulties. In Regina, my mother did not immediately feel the full effects of the economic collapse. In her case, they accumulated slowly over a period of three or four years, the withering consequences of financial and agrarian ruin visible only after she moved to the farm of her husband's family. She knew people lost their jobs, and wages plummeted for those who kept them. Earning very little money herself as a female domestic worker among the still well-to-do, who seemed able to withstand financial collapse but expressed fear over the future, Annie was indifferent to their anxieties. They spent more in a month than she made in a year. Without analyzing the causes, without articulating a plausible theory, she vaguely understood why John did not settle down. In many ways, they both fell victim to an overwhelming sense of homelessness. Not belonging anywhere, John rode the rails everywhere, easier to do in Canada in the twenties and thirties than it is today. Enchanted by Regina, Annie took the rattling streetcars to her cleaning jobs or walked. John hopped onto the boxcars, travelling as far as Timmins, Ontario, where he worked for a while in the mines.

He was not wandering the country seeking love and stability, nor did his movements bespeak the thrill of adventure and travel for travel's sake. Like Annie, he had lost the very foundations of his family life, but unlike Annie, his train rides from one place to another suggest that he didn't believe those foundations could ever be rebuilt. Having lost his first home, he did not seek another. Annie was incapable of understanding that brothers and sisters, however close as children, often wander out of each other's lives, their love for each other becoming more formality than feeling, their immediate friends and family becoming more significant than past relations. Despite the Romanian feeling for family, the biological connection does not always bind.

Recovering from their loss, my mother's sisters and her brother Nick each created new lives with new families. Annie may have realized how much she had in common with John when they went to the Dysart school together. As she shared her lunch with her brother and did his homework, her heart would break over the misery so plain on his face. As a boy, two years older than his sister, he did not elicit compassion and understanding from adults; his function in life was to behave and work. As long as there was work to be done, and work never ended on a farm, who cared about the sorrow in his soul over the death of his father and the loss of his family? Annie cared, without being able to put into words the concern she felt over her brother's future.

Despite her love, however, John paid little attention to his sister Annie. As an older brother, of course, he would have assumed all the cultural and social attitudes of males toward girls and women of the time. Their stories were not as compelling as his, their destinies locked up in marriage and babies. The open road and far horizons were not supposed to beckon women. True, more men rode the rails than women for whatever sociological and psychological reasons. As broken in heart as his sister, John worked (when he could find it) at miserable, dead-end jobs across the country and smoked himself into a cloud chamber. One of the lasting memories anyone had of brother John was his heavy addiction to tobacco. Annie sensed that John did not love her as much as she loved him, but she refused to acknowledge the fact.

News of his dreadful accident aroused all her concern. If she could cradle his head in her arms (how much he looked like her father in her memory), she could effect a cure. Believing that love possessed medicinal qualities, Annie ruminated about how she would nurse her brother, if means and opportunity offered themselves. But that was little more than a fantasy designed to hide her feelings of inadequacy and possibly guilt. She had been unable to help John as a child. Something terrible had gone wrong—she had seen the beginning of it in the schoolyard, when John scuffed the dirt and moped under the tree during recess.

The accident could have occurred anywhere along the rails, the mainline and the spurs. John had not written the note himself, and although the writer informed the family that the injury had reached beyond the bone into the brain itself, the person chose not to identify John's location. His brain damaged, he would never be the same again, his speech and cognitive skills, as it turned out, impaired. But medical intervention had in fact saved her brother's life, and he recovered in a manner of speaking. But where? Where would he go? What would he do? How would he work and support himself? Especially now when everyone talked about the closing of the banks and the loss of their life savings and the employment opportunities that shrank daily at a fearsome rate.

Cultural attitudes toward the dispossessed, the economically deprived and the intellectually impaired being what they were several decades ago, the fact that John was essentially a hobo, a term more commonly used in the thirties than today, and now mentally defective, did not make for an endearing brother. Recovering from the accident in whatever town or city hospital that had stitched his skull together, John hopped the train cars again as soon as he was physically able, either indifferent to or unconscious of the consequences of the accident. As there were fewer jobs to be found by digging ore or knocking on factory doors, he acquired bits and pieces of poorly paid work wherever the trains took him, until one day he returned to Regina and knocked on Tenka's door.

Every hobo originally belonged to a family, and no doubt Canadian hoboes of the Depression also had siblings better off than they, although the Depression had driven many families out of their mortgages and into poverty. How many people happily welcomed their indigent and homeless brothers? Tenka, opening the door on McIntosh Street, where she moved in 1930, first expressed dismay, quickly followed by distaste. A woman of propriety and property, the effects of the Depression on her life economically hard but not devastating, Tenka responded in a way that was shared by thousands across the country. John embodied a social nightmare and a walking reminder of potential disaster facing everyone. Embarrassed, her heart nonetheless touched by John's plight, she neither welcomed nor rejected her brother. Everything about him violated her sense of decorum and deportment, health, cleanliness and responsibility.

For one thing, John smelled of cow dung and piss, of tobacco smoke and unwashed clothes, of too many miles sleeping in boxcars designed to transport livestock and too few days with proper sustenance. His breath, fetid in the extreme, suggested an empty, acid-corroded stomach, and his decaying teeth, mostly hidden by an unkempt and dirty beard, added to the foul odours of his body. His hands scarred and callused, his nails bitten down to the flesh, his face furrowed and splotched from overexposure to severe sun and frostbiting cold, his brown eyes somewhat glazed over with a look of desperation and hopelessness, his hair greasy and unbrushed, he did not invite the loving embrace.

Annie, shouting John's name from behind her sister at the door, rushed to the threshold. Without stopping to criticize, she hugged her brother and kissed him full on the lips like Flaubert's Julian kissing the leper. Spontaneous love has little time for second thoughts. Only afterwards did Annie feel sick to her stomach and rinse out her mouth. She was about to lead him into the house when Tenka blocked the door. John could not enter her home. He was told to stay on the back porch, which was covered.

My uncle John didn't even have the sense he was born with to wash himself, my mother said, until she realized after staying with him on the porch for a time that he possessed little sense of himself at all. She experienced a double shock caused by loss compounded and dreams dashed. Shocked to see her brother in such a state, shocked to see that he didn't respond to her the way she had imagined he would. John let Annie hug him, but he failed to return the embrace, nor did he remember who she was except in a vague kind of way. Her dream had been the reunification of her family, and if God had a hand in it, here was John, muttering to himself behind a sticky growth of a beard, barely acknowledging his sister, although he mentioned Nick's name, to all intents and purposes deranged by the Devil.

He wasn't crazy, he was damaged. The Devil hadn't done it, John had done it to himself. Who told him to jump on to boxcars like an animal? Coming close to blaming and criticizing her brother when he was in dire need, a tendency she had to fight to suppress most of her life, Annie shrugged off her feelings of grievance and tried to think what was best for her brother at the moment. Without medical knowledge, without financial power, without influence of any kind except memory and yearning, she could do nothing except talk to him about the little boy whom she had met at recess time and encouraged to be brave, for they would soon be together again. And so they were, for a time, together on that little covered porch under the prairie sky. God was indeed great.

Annie went into the house to fetch a towel and pail of water to wash the man on the porch who had broken his crown. She fought against tears because they would have been more for herself than for her brother. She had learned that self-pity did not improve the day, just as hope never changed the weather. Going through the motions of washing her brother's face and hands, averting her face to catch a breath of fresh air, feeling as if she were preparing a body for the funeral, she realized then that it was impossible to regain what she had lost.

Tenka brought out a bowl of bean soup, cold *mămăligă*,

sausage and cheese, a blanket and a pillow. John could sleep on the porch that night. Annie encouraged her brother to eat, her heart broken over his failure to understand who she was. She talked about the times they had splashed about together in the shallows of the sloughs. When she mentioned her father's name, John did not seem to remember.

He ate hurriedly. After finishing the meal, he lay down on the floor and closed his eyes. Annie placed the pillow under his head and covered him with the blanket, holding her nose against the foul body odours. How he had come to be in that condition she did not fully comprehend. She had seen people shifting about on the streets before, people with no fixed address or steady job, and for the most part they had been pleasant enough and certainly cleaner than her brother. Was it the accident? Had it knocked every sense of self-regard out of John's mind? She didn't know.

She slept badly that night, occasionally returning to the porch to see if John was comfortable or awake and needed anything, until she fell asleep herself in the early hours of the morning. When she woke up, Tenka told her that John had left as suddenly as he had arrived. Washing the blanket and pillowcase he had used overnight, Tenka said she had given him a few dollars, money she could ill afford to spare, and their brother Nick's address. If there was a train to Truax that he could hop, he would probably go there. John seemed to have a stronger memory of Nick than he did of Annie.

To be so bitterly disappointed, she had to have loved her brother very much. A lingering stench reminded her of his presence, quickly blown away by the prairie breeze. She stood on the porch a long time, forgetting that she had a house to clean that morning, trying to stave off the depression that threatened to block her breathing. Her depressions often occurred for no apparent reason, but events could stir up melancholy. Without therapy and drugs, she needed all her psychic energies simply to focus on specific tasks. She would not let John's misery throw her into despair, although her appalling heaviness of spirit was like a stone in her heart.

She had wanted to run after her brother and even, for a moment, imagined the possibility of riding the rails with him, but her own nature revolted against the notion. Her belief in family depended on land and settlement, not on constant dislocation. How was it possible to live and love together when no one stood still? How long she remained on the porch Annie did not know, but she was fired from the household later that day for failing to show up for work. Tenka refused to talk about her brother; she had her own life and family to look after. The Depression wasn't making life any easier. For Annie, losing a job should have been cause for grief, but in a city of many houses and a workforce of cheap labour, cheaper by the week as more and more workers queued up at the employment offices, there were still people who could pay someone else to scrub their toilet. Annie found another housecleaning job soon enough and passed a year or two forcing herself to complete the chores. Tenka's children helped to pull her out of the muck of inertia. Events occur and pass, but chronic depression is an event that does not pass; it only subsides. One's choice in the pre-Prozac era was clear, if not always possible to make, but Annie tried not to spiral too much inward and down. She learned to focus on the immediate, unalterable facts and necessities of daily living. Diapers had to be changed, floors washed, food prepared, laundry hung, shirts ironed: not inspiring work, but life-saving.

One day, more news arrived from Nick. Annie by then had learned to quash her expectations. The soaring heart, like Icarus, falters in mid-flight and sinks. Annie understood that no cushion would have softened the blow of another disappointment, so, caging her emotions and refusing to fly, she responded with hesitation, unwilling to allow herself to feel joy at the promise of reuniting with her brother Nick. Since his departure from the porch two or three years ago, she had heard nothing of John. Many a night she had wakened on hearing the howl of the freight train in the night, perhaps the loneliest sound in Canada.

Suddenly out of the blue prairie sky, Nick wrote and sent money for a train ticket to Truax. The suddenness was more apparent than real, because some thought had gone into inviting his sister Annie to stay with his family. My mother was beginning to feel like the stereotypical unmarried sister and convenient aunt who could be called on to manage her nieces and nephews. Not having a home of her own, she was ripe for the exploitation by her siblings, although kindly meant. Nick's wife seemed to have been suffering from debilitating ill health. Would Annie consider visiting them for a while and helping with the children?

A woman turned twenty, Annie boarded the train, leaving an exciting young city erected on ancient buffalo hunting grounds. Covering her melancholy with a thin layer of agreeability and good cheer, for she instinctively learned techniques of disguise and deception because no one wanted to know about depression, Annie arranged herself as comfortably as possible on the wooden seat of the train, a basket of food on her lap to take to her brother's house, and remembered her first train journey from Dysart. She stared out the window, feeling that stone pressing on her heart as the city moved backward and the wheat fields, heavily ridged and furrowed, snow lying in strips and patches like laundry blown off the clothesline, parted like a muddy sea to let the black dragon through. The magnificent sky raced alongside the speeding train, whisking against the windowpane and Annie's weeping, crooked eye.

CHAPTER 19

The young woman who collapses
while dancing will soon be a bride.

The experience of living in someone else's house, tending to their needs, caring for their children, yearning at the same time for her own family had the effect of increasing Annie's sense of otherness and her desire for permanency and love. The loss of her first family and the migration from one home to another since Samson's death, from her stepmother's house to that of the kindly couple in Montana, then to her aunt's, then to her sister's and now to her brother's, developed into feelings of exile. The train ride to Truax, a Saskatchewan town like many others in the thirties, allowed Annie time to realize that at the age of twenty, she belonged nowhere. No matter how kind and loving her sister and her brother Nick, she remained a guest, a temporary visitor, a hanger-on, a useful presence but not centrally important to their lives. Nor did they understand the fragmentation of her own.

Memories of Sophie's ferocious attacks against her body and spirit kept assailing Annie's idea of self, and she doubted her own value. Try as she might, Annie could not forgive her aunt, the rage so thick that it swelled in her mind like storm clouds mounting over the horizon. Thinking back as the train sped forward, a small woman whose glossy black hair was kept off her face with bobby pins tucked in strategic places, averting her eyes from the other passengers because she preferred not to draw attention to herself or engage in conversation with strangers, Annie struggled against the impulse to cry in the corner of the seat.

She succeeded in the battle this time because the train journey was short. And the immediate sensation of greeting her brother in the Truax station prevented despair from forcing her hand in any unfortunate way. She was beginning to be troubled by frightening images, daydreams of herself in a coffin, arms crossed over her breast, hands clasping a bejewelled Byzantine cross, Aunt Sophie, stricken by grief and overwhelmed by guilt, on her knees and screaming at the edge of the flower-strewn grave. But Annie used common sense to control irrational impulses. Despite her anger and sorrow, she had acquired a redeeming sense of perspective. The Depression itself provided ample evidence of people at their wit's end, of men and women downtrodden and beaten back. No matter where she looked, she witnessed the fact that misery was a crowded place, standing room only. The knowledge that other people suffered offered her consolation.

And who was she to be unhappy when her brother Nick had two lovely children whom she could care for during their mother's illness? Fortunately, she enjoyed good health herself. In the 1930s, people like her brother John, dispossessed of home and employment, lined up in front of public bulletin boards posting job opportunities or they travelled like the Indians, who packed their belongings in single-horse-drawn wagons or creaky flatbed trucks and traipsed up and down the countryside looking for work in a land that used to be theirs. And Nick did at least, unlike John, return the embrace. Annie believed she cried from joy, but that may have been the wind in her eyes.

She was on her guard, though, having learned from both Tenka and John that not everyone felt the way she did. At this point in her life, Annie strengthened her reserve to prevent revealing to anyone how she felt. She went about her business with a quiet dedication and a remote attitude that was often mistaken for coldness. She hid her tremendous struggle to keep depression from destroying her waking hours, but it took its toll on her happiness and peace of mind. Here was another surrogate family to help deflect attention from the void inside her. My mother spoke rarely of the weeks she spent in her brother Nick's house. His daughter Connie provided release from the turmoil within and allowed Annie to express love without danger of its being rejected. She never spoke about her sister-in-law, who suffered poor health for years and died in childbirth at the age of thirty-nine in 1945. Her prematurely born baby girl died a year later. By that time, Annie had lost touch with her brother for the second time and was unaware of his personal tragedies.

She rarely mentioned her brother Nick, and when she did, Annie overlaid what she knew about his life with elements from other parts of her story. Decades later, heart heavy with her past, she often confused the two brothers and forgot, or chose to forget, that she had actually lived with Nick in Truax. She said that John had been killed by falling off a train, that Nick had run away and she had never seen him again or that he had never married and fathered children, even though many years later she received a visit from Connie. Facts and dates always stood on unsteady ground in Annie's memories, except for her horrendous years in Sophie's house, as if that experience overshadowed later events.

Her fatalistic view of the world, common to the peasantry, whereby the Devil tended to have more prominence in human affairs than religion allowed, began shaping, controlling and distorting her memories. Goodness by its very nature was transitory, and happiness such a fleeting emotion that she could scarcely hang on to it before it disappeared. Aunt Sophie remained vibrant and tangible in her mind, Nick chimerical and elusive.

Like most pessimists, Annie possessed a sense of humour that allowed her to endure the antics of children without resentment. A caring woman who loved to laugh and felt most at ease with the natural playfulness of the very young, she looked after the children well, as Nick's daughter, only four or five at the time, remembers. Making comparisons between what she desired and what her brother possessed, however, did not contribute to personal satisfaction. Once again, Annie remained on the outside looking in.

The prairie was so vast, but too small to afford a place Annie could call her own. During the Depression, when family after family lost their farms, banks foreclosed and savings evaporated, Annie's sense of dispossession became entangled with social circumstances. Everywhere, the ground shifted and people tumbled. Despair was visible; one could smell it in the very breath of the unemployed.

After living with Nick and his family for a few months, Annie did not hesitate to apply for a housekeeping job in Regina again. Nick had thanked my mother but was never aware of her longing for a home of her own. Why would he have been? Men were not expected to seek into the secret thoughts of women.

At a time of massive economic collapse, social concerns outweighed individual problems. People in the thirties were always adept at pointing out people who suffered more. Such comparisons always contained a hint of cold-hearted righteousness: how dare she complain when that family down the street no longer had a home to call their own and depended on soup kitchens for sustenance? She should consider herself lucky to find even a housekeeping job when able-bodied men could find nothing. Of course, Annie had never complained, for it is in the nature of the peasant mind to endure rather than to resist. Annie had learned the techniques of secrecy to prevent mockery. It was better to pretend than to reveal. It was also better to move again than to remain and be reminded of what she did not possess. Happiness in others was not a soothing balm for her soul.

She returned to Tenka's house, but not for long. Holding Tenka's daughter, Elaine, by the hand, she walked from her sister's residence on McIntosh Street to the nearest streetcar that would rattle and squeal its way as close as possible to her future place of employment in the 2100 block of Winnipeg Street. She wore her very best clothes, ones that actually fit properly. As an adult, she never appeared at any remotely official place or event—doctor's office, church or interview with a potential employer—without dressing as well as she could. It was important not to give the impression of neediness or despair. She remembered wearing a brown pleated skirt that reached down to her ankles, a crisply pressed white blouse with a round collar buttoned at the neck and a brown bouclé cardigan, all purchased, miracle of miracles, with her own money.

And, somewhat surprisingly, Annie found new living quarters. Meeting a pleasant couple at St. Nicholas', she discovered they had an extra room in their house that she could rent at an affordable cost. They lived on a farm not far from Regina where they attended church. Housekeeping did not pay much, but Annie would enjoy a few coins in her purse after paying the rent on her own room. If some light housekeeping and farm duties were also required, she would gladly give her time and effort. In any case, Annie could never sit still in a house if her eye spied a chore waiting to be done. Irene was broadly built like many Eastern European women of the era, several years older than Annie, with hair pinned and rolled into a tight bun at the back, forever caged in a net. My mother never saw Irene's hair unpinned. Only the net changed. For Sunday services and feast days in the *biserică*, gold flecks or silver stars glinted on Irene's head in the candlelit ceremonies of the church. Proud of the glossy luxuriance of her own hair, Annie did not cage it in a bun. Michael, Irene's husband, of slim build and gesticulating hands—they moved constantly—sported an improbable handlebar moustache, which he waxed every morning. Michael also enjoyed a local reputation as a marriage broker.

Although young Romanians met in the church, a bachelor did not always meet the appropriate young woman in the eyes of his family, and vice versa. A marriage broker kept records in his head of whose children had reached marriageable age, where they lived, the financial situation of their parents, their prospects and their character—although character was not the deciding factor. Romanian communities, scattered throughout central and southern Saskatchewan, were neither so remote nor too large for a marriage broker to travel from door to door, offering advice and pointing to likely candidates in exchange for a gift or a fee. If a man was single, employed, clean and came from a decent family, much was overlooked in his character. Deficient personality or defective intelligence could be compensated for by the promise of inheritance or a willingness to work.

Annie had always been too shy to put herself forward and too unappealing to approach. If that lessened her chances in the marriage market—for it was a kind of barter-and-exchange affair passing through the adroit hands of the broker—there was no help for it. Of course, the idea of marriage appealed to my mother. She did not belong to a generation that offered many options to women. But she had nothing to give except her dedication and body. If her notion of sexuality derived from activities on the farm, she wasn't entirely misinformed about relations between men and women. And she did so want a baby of her own.

Romance was not a factor, although traditionally a young man and young woman met in the presence of chaperones or parents, then had time to court. No one expected people to fall in love. Love at first sight in the Shakespearean sense was possible but did not afflict my mother, whose reserve was too great. Michael had arranged several introductions that had led to successful marriages, blessed by the parents. Look, how happy the couples were, carrying babies to the church, the wife serving her husband at the dinners in the church hall. Annie should give marriage some thought. She wasn't getting any younger. Did she want to spend the rest of her life as a boarder in someone else's house, an unmarried woman with no children of her own to care for, no grandchildren—Mother of God, how would she live?

No, Annie did not wish to live in someone else's house for the rest of her life. When news reached them again about John, who this time showed up at Nick's house, Annie did not rush to embrace her brother. She had picked up the odour of rejection that day on the back porch, when she saw her brother only through her fantasies. Her story that he had actually died on the train tracks became fixed, and though she knew what had actually happened to him, she chose not to tell the truth.

Shortly after Michael introduced Annie to Serban, her future husband, Tenka informed her that John was suffering from tuberculosis, a still devastating and rampant disease in the early decades of the century. Fort Qu'Appelle, for example, only a short distance from Dysart, boasted a sanatorium, if "boast" is the right word, locally known as "the San." Still standing, it is now used as a convention centre. John's illness rendered him incapable of riding the rails anymore or of working, so he was institutionalized in the tuberculosis hospital in North Battleford, where he died in 1935 or 1936.

Nick travelled by bus to visit his dying twenty-four-year-old brother; Annie did not. So, this restless, unemployed man, a child of Romanian immigrants, devastated by the death of his parents and the separation of his siblings, knocked off his feet by the Depression, his lungs ravaged by consumption, perished. Annie prayed for John in the St. Nicholas *biserică*, although religion no longer moved her heart. She went through the rituals by rote rather than by faith. Hope, not belief, made her light a candle in her brother's name.

CHAPTER 20

Paper is harder than stone.

Drought and heat dried the sloughs and sucked up the moisture from the depths of the soil and cracked the landscape in parts of Saskatchewan. Topsoil that had not baked under the unrelenting sun whirled up in the winds and blew away. Rain fell sporadically, unevenly, favouring one region over another. The Assiniboia district in southwest Saskatchewan, for example, especially suffered from lack of rain, more than the Qu'Appelle Valley, whose five lakes among the hills did not evaporate. Still remembering the quasi-Edenic world of the Dysart and Qu'Appelle Valley area of her childhood, Annie made the unconscious mistake of assuming farmers in one area were more adept than those in another, that rainfall was the result of agricultural skill rather than weather patterns. She knew perfectly well that dry weather in winter and summer—for snow is as important to the prairie farmer as rain—financial failure, plagues of grasshoppers and other insects all contributed to defeat a great many people, however courageous their struggle to survive.

Her views did not originate from mere ignorance—of life on the farm Annie was not ignorant—but from disappointment. The beauty of her childhood farm remained the ideal geographic picture of what a farm was supposed to be. Anything less she attributed to human deficiency, not the forces of nature.

Moreover, her siblings, associated in her mind with the loveliness of the land, became semi-magical creatures in her imagination, possessed of the power to liberate her from the sorrows of the world and help her recover the lost garden.

One night not long after John's death, Annie walked along the grid road that ran beside Michael and Irene's property until she came to the intersection where it met the main highway to Regina. They had enjoyed a cream-of-chicken supper in the kitchen. Irene and Michael had retired to their parlour to listen to their new radio. The land around Regina is flatter than it is near Annie's childhood home, and it was possible from the farm to get a view of the city in the distance. The proposal was accepted, and their wedding date set for July, two months away, unless Serban's family found reason to protest. Irene said they would be happy; Annie was not to worry.

A solitary figure on the road approached Annie from the west. Under the clear, starlit sky, she enjoyed an excellent view in the dark, the moon so bright that it cast shadows on the land. Less afraid now than she would have been a few years earlier, Annie felt no apprehension, did not wince under the rush of timidity that had often left her tongue-tied in the presence of strangers. She knew by the dress that the figure was Native, perhaps a Cree. Only Indian women still wore those heavy-skirted, ankle-length dresses, hand-me-downs and cast-offs from the pre-war years. Although the nights could be chilly in early May, it wasn't cold, and she wondered why the woman also had a scarf wrapped around her neck as if to ward off the winter's icy wind. Perhaps she was ill.

Where did she belong, this woman? The closest reserve was some distance away and none of the neighbouring farms was owned by Indians. Perhaps she was a hired hand, although Annie didn't think a farmer would hire such an old woman. Did she enjoy walking the country roads at night? Was she visiting relatives? Judging by the creases in the brown face, Annie imagined that the woman must have lived a hundred years exposed to the weather of the prairie. In the white light of the moon the old woman's eyes looked dark and distant, absorbing the light. Whatever thoughts she possessed could not be read. She stopped to stare at Annie, then began to speak.

She did not speak English. At first Annie thought the old woman was extending her hand for money or food, but she didn't seem to be begging. The hand was twisted and knotty like the bark of a dead tree, the fingernails black. Annie couldn't see teeth. Annie asked the old woman's name, but the response was incomprehensible. Where was she going, where had she come from?

The moon shone directly on the old woman's face. Annie had never seen such an old face, could not even begin to imagine that this woman had once been young. Had she at one time been crowned in a wedding ceremony? Where were her children? Why was she walking alone? Then Annie remembered hearing or reading that among certain Native groups old people, not to be a burden to their communities, were either left to die or voluntarily walked out of the village in search of their final resting place. Was it possible this old woman was looking for a place to die? Annie shivered at the intersection, frightened by what she perceived as an image of loneliness and irrelevance. To live so long and end up walking alone under the moon in a world that was no longer hers. She tightened the cardigan around her, for the night had grown cooler.

To resist depression, Annie had doubled her household efforts that past week, scouring what had already been cleaned the day before, baking more bread than was required and successfully stretching *plăcintă* dough so thin that she could see her lifeline beneath it. The efforts didn't entirely succeed because one night Annie had allowed herself to sit for a long period in the outhouse and cry. She stopped only when she heard Irene calling to her from the house. Without being able to point to a specific cause for her sadness, she blamed it on anxiety.

Old woman, she wanted to ask, tell me what will happen, believing that age conferred wisdom, and that Native women, by scattering bones, could read the future. Well, no bones were immediately available, but the woman was so ancient that she also had to be wise beyond compare. The woman's hair, uncovered, unbraided, unfeathered, spread like a full grey cape over her nape and across her back. The moon shone on the silver-and-white strands. Before Annie could speak, the old woman touched her shoulder.

Startled by the gesture, which felt like the reassuring caress of a mother, Annie said nothing. For a long moment, with the moon travelling across the sky and the stars so plentiful that they were like flecks of diamonds, Annie and the Native woman stared at each other. Then the woman dropped her arm, turned and continued down the road. Annie did not call after her but watched until the figure disappeared in the moonlight. The road, devoid of humanity, glinted in the starry night.

Epilogue

Sarmale (Cabbage Rolls)

3 pounds ground meat (pork, beef and/or veal)
1¼ cups cooked rice
1 large onion, diced
1 tablespoon vegetable oil or shortening
1½ teaspoons salt
1 teaspoon black pepper
1 tablespoon paprika
28-ounce can stewed tomatoes
¼ teaspoon dried chili pepper
1 large cabbage

- In a pot, brown onion in oil, then mix with meat, rice, salt, pepper, paprika and 1 cup of tomatoes.
- Parboil cabbage and remove leaves.
- Roll some meat mixture in each leaf, folding in ends.
- Line bottom of large pot with chopped leftover pieces from centre of cabbage.
- Arrange rolls in pot and add remaining tomatoes with dried chilies.
- Bring to boil and simmer for 1 to 1½ hours.

Serves 10–12.

Epilogue

During my childhood and well into adulthood, I heard the full drama of Annie's early life rolling out of her mind with the skilful ease of the wooden rolling pin flattening the dough on the table. After I had left home, returning for visits, we continued more or less where we left off, as if the narrative had never been interrupted. There were areas of her autobiography she did not touch on, equally momentous events in her married life she refused to speak about, even to the point of imagining they had never happened. She kept focusing on her early life, a technique I now recognize as a means of avoiding things she could not bring herself to reveal, although she wanted to unburden her heart through the art and act of telling. I also think she wanted to re-establish a sense of her unique self, Annie as a complex, separate person, before she disappeared under the roles of wife and mother.

After unpacking and putting food away, the kettle on the stove for tea, a dish of strudel or homemade bread with jam, I sat at the table, eating and drinking, as my mother washed and wrenched apart a chicken for stew. The stories began, sometimes prompted by my asking, more often picked out of the midstream of her memory. Generally, we were alone, my older brothers and sisters having gone out for the day or preoccupying themselves with other things. My willingness to listen—bribed by food and fascinated—and my status as the youngest child still attached to his mother perhaps allowed me to be the audience Annie unconsciously needed. She spoke in a low voice, often chuckling, the humour tinged with bitter irony, repeating what she had previously said, adding a detail, veering off into unexpected directions, collapsing chronology and eliding events, new facts sometimes contradicting old.

Annie repeated the stories, reliving some of the worst moments to the verge of tears, sometimes laughing. She was shaping her story, asserting her voice, situating herself in the world and, as usual, feeding a child. Toward the end of her life, when her body was decrepit, her spirit exhausted from decades of psychological struggle, her houseplants still flourishing, little more than a few tomato plants and a rose bush or two in her garden, I sat at her chrome kitchen table, drinking tea and eating her miraculous strudel, sensing the urgency in her words: "You write this," she used to say, twisting the handkerchief, "you write this."

Acknowledgments

Thanks to my editor, Iris Tupholme, who knew there was another story, and to my agent, Denise Bukowski, for her sense of direction.

The staff of the National Archives in Ottawa were always courteous and helpful, as were the good people of the Saskatchewan Archives (Regina), the Saskatchewan Genealogical Society Library and the Prairie History Room of the Regina Public Library. Thanks also to Jo-Anne Colby of the Canadian Pacific Railway Archives and to Don Ryback of the Commercial Weather Services Division of Environment Canada.

I wish to express my gratitude to Stephen Gherasim of the St. George Romanian Orthodox Church in Dysart, Saskatchewan, and Vera Gherasim, for their cooperation, stories and hospitality; to Hertha Wilson of Lipton, Saskatchewan, for sharing her memories; and to Gladys Petrar of the Dysart Heritage Society for her kind assistance.

For telling me the stories and facts they knew, thanks go to my cousins Elaine Maiers and Connie Morgan. It's also a pleasure to acknowledge the help offered by my sister Elaine and my brother John, both of whom provided family documents and pictures.

Many thanks to Alison Reid and Rebecca Vogan for their sensitive copyediting and proofreading.

Without the research skills, encouragement and organizational genius of my wife, Diane, this work would not have been possible.